Malcolm Duncan is Lead Pastor at Dundonald Elim Church, a Pentecostal church located in Belfast, Northern Ireland. He is Chair of Elim's Ethics and Public Theology Task Force and Theologian-in-Residence for Spring Harvest and Essential Christian.

T0018272

FLIPPED

Life in the upside-down kingdom

Malcolm Duncan

First published in Great Britain in 2023

Society for Promoting Christian Knowledge
36 Causton Street
London SW1P 4ST
www.spck.org.uk

Copyright © Spring Harvest 2023

Malcolm Duncan has asserted his right under the Copyright, Designs and Patents Act,
1988, to be identified as Author of this work.

All rights reserved. No part of this book may be reproduced or transmitted in any
form or by any means, electronic or mechanical, including photocopying, recording, or
by any information storage and retrieval system, without permission in writing from
the publisher.

SPCK does not necessarily endorse the individual views contained in its publications.

The author and publisher have made every effort to ensure that the external website and
email addresses included in this book are correct and up to date at the time of going to
press. The author and publisher are not responsible for the content, quality or continuing
accessibility of the sites.

British Library Cataloguing-in-Publication Data
A catalogue record for this book is available from the British Library

ISBN 978-0-281-08812-6
eBook ISBN 978-0-281-08813-3

1 3 5 7 9 10 8 6 4 2

Typeset by Fakenham Prepress Solutions, Fakenham, Norfolk NR21 8NL
First printed in Great Britain by Clays Ltd

eBook by Fakenham Prepress Solutions, Fakenham, Norfolk NR21 8NL

Produced on paper from sustainable sources

Contents

Dedication and thanks

This book is dedicated to the late John Lancaster and the late John Smyth, my principal at Bible College and fellow Ulsterman.

Heroes and friends, who will never be forgotten.

I also dedicate it to my wife, Debbie – thank you for all you do and all you are; to my children and their spouses and partner – Matthew and Eve, Benjamin and Ellie, Anna and Jacob and Riodhna and Matt; and to my four grand-children – Arthur, Caleb, Leo and Penelope. May you change the world for Christ.

Lastly, I dedicate this to the family at Dundonald Elim Church and to my Spring Harvest family. What a journey we are on and what a joy to be on it with you all.

Thank you to Elizabeth Neep and Wendy Grisham at SPCK, to Nicki Copeland for her careful copy editing of the manuscript, and to the Spring Harvest team for your continued support, encouragement and love. Thank you for your patience and understanding, and your tireless work. It is a privilege to work with you all and to minister alongside you.

The writing of this book was impacted by the death of my brother, the Covid pandemic, the death of Her Majesty Queen Elizabeth II and the heartbreaking events in Donegal in the autumn of 2022.

An invitation: learning to live again

So the last will be first, and the first will be last.
Jesus (as quoted in Matthew 20.16)

The warm, fragrant air of Bangladesh wrapped itself around me like a blanket of hopeful expectation as I stepped off the plane and made my way towards the bus that was waiting on the tarmac. My tiredness from the flight was overcome by the sense of antici-pation that I felt rising in my spirit at the prospect of my visit to this remarkable country with its resilient, hospitable and humble people.

I knew that this trip, like others I had taken before it, would change me. It did, as have many others that I have taken since. They have taught me that God's kingdom is flipped. In it the first are last and the last are first. The powerful are made to wait in line and the dispossessed are brought to the front of the queue. The trappings of success and influence and power are stripped away, and the heart is shown. It is a kingdom where the forgotten are remembered, the lost are found, the excluded are welcomed in, the impoverished are enriched, the discounted are counted, the silenced are heard, the ignored are noticed, the grieving are comforted, the weak are given strength, the foolish are endowed with wisdom and the oppressed are liberated.

That is what this book is about – being flipped – life in the upside-down kingdom of God.

As I looked around at my fellow travellers arriving in Bangladesh that day, I wondered why they had made the journey. Having chatted to some people during the flight, I knew the motivation behind a few of those leaving the plane with me. One man in his mid-thirties was returning home to the embrace of loved ones and to laughter-soaked, joy-laden reunions after nearly fifteen years away. His family had sent him to the UK for an education and to secure a job and a future, not just for himself but also for them. An older lady was making a farewell journey for a recently deceased family member. Her pilgrimage home would also involve the selling of a piece of land, the closing-up of a family home and the transition to a new chapter in their unfolding story.

Why was I stepping onto the bus? What had drawn me to this beautiful, bustling nation with its colour and vibrancy?

Ostensibly, I was coming to Bangladesh to support, encourage and teach leaders in the Christian church in Dhaka, the country's capital located pretty much centrally in terms of geography, and then to do the same in Rangpur in the north, in Sylhet in the east and in Chattogram in the south. If we had time, we would head to Rajshahi in the west of the country, but that was not yet confirmed. I was scheduled to explore pastoral ethics with church leaders and to explore the connections between mission and justice, evangelism and community action, and to teach overviews of the Hebrew Bible and the New Testament. Leaders from local churches would travel to locations in each part of the country where we would spend a few days together in the hope that God would use the time:

> to equip the saints for the work of the ministry, for building up the body of Christ, until all of us come to the unity of the faith and of the knowledge of the Son of God, to maturity, to the measure of the full stature of Christ.
> (Ephesians 4.12–13)

The trip did achieve these aims and objectives, but it did so much more. It confronted me with the reality that God's economy is not the same as ours, and God's way of doing things is not only different from our way of doing things, but also often at odds with our way of doing things.

I was picked up by a driver at the airport and, as we emerged into the teeming life of Dhaka, the car was swamped with children. They banged on the doors, they hit the windows. To be honest, it felt like a mob had surrounded us. They were begging. As they pleaded with us in the vehicle to give them something, I noticed that many of the children (mostly boys) had hands missing. Some of them had both hands missing. Some of the children looked like they had lost an eye. Some had whole limbs missing. This was my first visit to Bangladesh, and I was taken aback by the sheer volume of children begging and shocked by the high number of physical impairments they were displaying. My driver explained that these were some of the street children of Dhaka. Their disabilities were not genetic; they were inflicted on them by women and men who view them as human cashpoints.

I would later learn that there are around 600,000 such children in Bangladesh. Around 380,000 of them are aged between five and 14 and more than half live in Dhaka. The pavement is their bed and the sky their roof, and they are always vulnerable to predators. Some are trafficked, some are taken into gangs and mutilated so that those from whom they beg will be more charitable and give more. They rarely get to keep the money they receive from their begging, it being passed on to their owners or handlers. Those who aren't owned are often the breadwinners in their families. I often see their faces when I pray.

The kingdom of God belongs to such as these

I have encountered similar scenes in many countries around the world. From Phnom Penh in Cambodia to San Salvador in El Salvador; from Beira in Mozambique to Kigali in Rwanda, I have been reminded that the kingdom of God belongs not to the great and the good, but to people who have counted themselves out and to those who are serving and helping them. It has often been in the lives of children and those supporting them that I have seen this truth most clearly. Jesus told us as much:

> Then little children were being brought to him in order that he might lay his hands on them and pray. The disciples spoke sternly to those who brought them; but Jesus said, 'Let the little children come to me, and do not stop them; for it is to such as these that the kingdom of heaven belongs.'
> (Matthew 19.13–15)

Over the days of that first trip to Bangladesh, I was confronted with the reality of God's kingdom again and again. I heard the hope and the resilience of many of these children in their laughter or their excited chatter or their whoops of excitement as some of the teams I was visiting helped them. I wept as I watched dispossessed and poor women and men in the teams that I was working with share their very little with these children and their families. The occasional visitor, like me, would come and do a little to help, but when we did, we were invariably confronted with the uncomfortable challenge that God does not see ministry in the same was as many of us do. I have discovered that I carry very little to the table in ministry. I learn far more than I teach. I discover far more than I deposit. I receive far more than I give. I find far more than I bring. This is not only true in global mission; it is true also in all mission and all ministries.

I became a Christian in 1986 in Belfast during The Troubles and have been involved in formal local church and broader 'ministry' since 1988. I am a pastor–theologian, a preacher and a leader. I've led charities and churches. I'm involved in mission and ministry every day of my life. I have travelled the world and sat with some of the most powerful women and men on the planet. I have also sat with some of the most excluded, overlooked and forgotten. I have learned far more about God's kingdom in the homes of the hurting and in the pain of the unfairly treated than I have in the corridors of power and the cabinet rooms of the governing. The bedraggled and the broken, of whom I am one, have bejewelled my life and my understanding with the beauty of life in the upside-down kingdom.

Through my encounters and over the years, my definitions of ministry, church, leadership, worship, encounter, discipleship, prayer, giving, faithfulness, orthodoxy, orthopraxy, unity, anointing, empowerment by the Spirit, witness, mission, community, sacrifice, commitment, intercession, prosperity, success, endurance, suffering, faith, generosity, hope, despair, trust, loss, victory, failure, beauty, preaching, teaching and just about everything else you could imagine have been changed. Very often, what I have been taught about ministry and about being a Christian has been brought into sharp conflict with what I have seen in the lives of Christians who are faithfully living out their calling in ways that are richer, clearer and more authentic than my own.

Where I have often been taught, trained and conditioned for the purposes of building and strengthening a congregation or a denomination or a Christian cause, the people I have encountered who have changed me and my thinking have been partnering with their Creator in building the kingdom of God (often when they did not know it themselves). They have understood that this is the purpose of the church. This is not dualism; it is holism. It is a deeply rooted understanding that the church is an agent of God's kingdom, not the other way round. Let me give you just two examples.

We meet God in the lives of the poor – epiphany in a Vauxhall Cavalier

I spent a year as a pastor in Somerset in the 1990s. It ended far quicker than I would have anticipated, but it taught me far more than I could ever explain.

5

James (not his real name) was addicted to heroin. He came to live with me and my wife after turning up at our church building one Sunday morning and asking for help. We were blessed and privileged to get to know him a little bit. He had been brought up in a strict religious family but had gone off the rails as a teenager because he got caught up with the wrong crowd and was drawn into a lifestyle of drug taking, theft and violence. In the end, his habit stripped him of his sense of dignity, worth and purpose. He sold himself to feed his habit.

His life ended while he was with us because of a mistaken administration of methadone (a controlled replacement for heroin), when a prescription was read incorrectly and he was given far more methadone than he should have had. It was an error. No one did it on purpose. My wife and I and the few people who had got to know him were devasted at such a tragic waste of life and possibility.

Yet in the last few months of his life we had witnessed a transformation that is hard to describe. James went from feeling unwanted and unnoticed to lifting his head, knowing he was loved and beginning to believe that he had a future. He knew God loved him. He knew his family loved him. He knew that a little community in our church loved him. He knew that he was not defined by his sin, his mistakes or his habit, but that he was defined as an Image-Bearer of God, a child of the King.

He found hope.

One Saturday night before James died, our church treasurer was holding a barbecue in his home and he invited us to come. 'Bring James', he said. 'We'd love to have him.'

So I did. Debbie, my wife, was unable to attend for some reason I can no longer remember, so James and I travelled together in my car. It was an old blue Vauxhall Cavalier that someone had generously given to us because we had no money, and our previous car had been falling apart. I was so very proud of that car, and so very, very grateful for it.

We had a great evening at the barbecue. James loved it. New friendships were being formed, new pathways opening for him. He smiled all night. And he ate a lot! I was witnessing what it looked like for someone to be 'born again' (John 3.3 NIVUK). His whole life was starting again. This transformation wasn't brought about by a massive rehabilitation programme, or by thousands and thousands of people and millions of pounds. It was happening because a small group of individuals noticed James.

We saw him.

We listened to him.

We loved him.

We made space for him in our lives.

We were simply doing what Jesus had told his disciples he would bless.

When the Son of Man comes in his glory, and all the angels with him, then he will sit on the throne of his glory. All the nations will be gathered before him, and he will separate people one from another as a shepherd separates the sheep from the goats, and he will put the sheep at his right hand and the goats at the left. Then the king will say to those at his right hand, 'Come, you that are blessed by my Father, inherit the kingdom prepared for you from the foundation of the world; for I was hungry and you gave me food, I was thirsty and you gave me something to drink, I was a stranger and you welcomed me, I was naked and you gave me clothing, I was sick and you took care of me, I was in prison and you visited me.' Then the righteous will answer him, 'Lord, when was it that we saw you hungry and gave you food, or thirsty and gave you something to drink? And when was it that we saw you a stranger and welcomed you, or naked and gave you clothing? And when was it that we saw you sick or in prison and visited you?' And the king will answer them, 'Truly I tell you, just as

you did it to one of the least of these who are members of my family, you did it to me.'
(Matthew 25.31–40)

All of us who knew James were far more blessed by him than we were a blessing to him. I do not mean that our love and commitment to him was trivial – that is not at all the case. Loving him was not always easy. After all, when God begins to straighten our crooked lines, we all feel it a little and lash out. As God began bending James back into shape, it was a painful process for him, and that pain sometimes showed itself in the way he treated others – but it was worth it.

Something happened to me, and only to me, with James that was remarkable, however. I return to it again and again.

The night of the barbecue, as we were driving away, James was in the passenger seat of my blue Vauxhall Cavalier, and I was driving. I was taking him home – he had secured a place in a great 'halfway house' with terrific support. We were chatting in the car, and I asked him how he had found the evening. He told me he had loved it. He went quiet for a moment; I knew that emotion had overcome him, and I let the silence linger – you should not always be loud in the presence of the holy – then he said to me, quietly and tearfully, 'Malcolm, for the first time in my life I feel like I have hope again and that I am part of a family.'

It was a beautiful moment, a God-soaked, grace-laden, heavy-with-hope moment. I turned to look at James for a second.

Jesus was looking back at me.

I cannot explain it. I had never encountered anything like it before and have not encountered anything like it in quite the same way since. This was a kingdom moment in which God, the Holy Spirit, flooded my soul and reached into the very centre of my being. I was undone. I had to pull over in the car, and simply sit. James was still James, and I was still me, but we both knew that God

8

was present in this powerful moment. Our Creator was meeting with us. God was meeting with me, and God was doing it through the life of a poor man. My Saviour was coming to me in the eyes of a new Christian who was coming off heroin. James had nothing and yet he had everything.

This is what the kingdom looks like. I, the teacher, was being flipped into being the learner. I, the giver, was being flipped into being the receiver. I, the host, was made the guest. I, the leader, was being led. I, the one blessed with resources and family, was confronted with my own poverty and lack. God meets us in the lives of the poor – this is the upside-down nature of life in the flipped kingdom.

I later found words to describe this reality in the work of Gustavo Gutiérrez, the Peruvian theologian of liberation: 'Christ hides himself behind the faces of those whom we tend to avoid because they have little importance in the eyes of society,' he wrote.[1] To be a follower of Jesus, for Gutiérrez, requires us to walk with and commit ourselves to the poor. In doing so, we encounter the Lord 'who is simultaneously revealed and hidden in the face of the Poor'.[2] To serve someone who is poor is to serve God in Christ. Gutiérrez wrote that 'we find God in our encounter with others, especially the poor, marginalized, and exploited ones. An act of love toward them is an act of love toward God.'[3] He was convinced that:

> Our encounter with the Lord occurs in our encounter with others, especially in encounter with those whose human features have been disfigured by oppression, despoliation, and alienation and who have 'no beauty, no majesty' but are the things from which men turn away their eyes.[4]

To be converted *to* God is to also to be drawn into direct relationship with the poor – it is to be converted *to* the poor as well. Describing this as a theology of liberation, Gutiérrez wrote that 'a spirituality of liberation will enter on a conversion to neighbour, the oppressed person, the exploited social class, the despised ethnic group, the dominated country. Our conversion to the Lord implies this conversion to the neighbour.'[5]

My encounter with God in my Vauxhall Cavalier was an encounter with God through James. It enfleshed a reality that Jesus articulated:

> When the Pharisees heard that he had silenced the Sadducees, they gathered together, and one of them, a lawyer, asked him a question to test him. 'Teacher, which commandment in the law is the greatest?' He said to him, '"You shall love the Lord your God with all your heart, and with all your soul, and with all your mind." This is the greatest and first commandment. And a second is like it: "You shall love your neighbour as yourself." On these two commandments hang all the law and the prophets.'
> (Matthew 22.34–40)

I cannot love God without loving my neighbour. God comes to meet us in the lives of those around us, and if we are to love God, we must love those around us. Not only is this true, but the implication of this reality is that to encounter God we must encounter our neighbour, and the Scriptures make clear that our neighbour is the person in need right in front of us, whoever and wherever they are. To illustrate this point, Luke's gospel places the parable of the Good Samaritan immediately after Jesus' command to love God and love our neighbour.

> Jesus replied with a story: 'A Jewish man was traveling from Jerusalem down to Jericho, and he was attacked by bandits. They stripped him of his clothes, beat him up, and left him half dead beside the road.

'By chance a priest came along. But when he saw the man lying there, he crossed to the other side of the road and passed him by. A Temple assistant walked over and looked at him lying there, but he also passed by on the other side.

'Then a despised Samaritan came along, and when he saw the man, he felt compassion for him. Going over to him, the Samaritan soothed his wounds with olive oil and wine and bandaged them. Then he put the man on his own donkey and took him to an inn, where he took care of him. The next day he handed the innkeeper two silver coins, telling him, "Take care of this man. If his bill runs higher than this, I'll pay you the next time I'm here."

'Now which of these three would you say was a neighbour to the man who was attacked by bandits?' Jesus asked.

The man replied, 'The one who showed him mercy.'

Then Jesus said, 'Yes, now go and do the same.'

(Luke 10.30–37, NLT)

James taught me that in seeing the poor, the dispossessed and the disadvantaged, I see God. He was neither the first nor the last person to show me that, but my encounter with the Holy Spirit through my encounter with him made sense of the times, before that moment, when I had met God in the lives of others. It has also given meaning to the encounters that I have had with God through the poor since that moment.

As I look across my entire life, not just since I was converted in 1986, I can pinpoint moments when I have encountered God in the lives of those who are considered less or are viewed as poor. For years, I could not give language or definition to these encounters and what they meant, but now I can.

I met God on the streets of Istanbul in the outstretched hand of a beggar when I was 11 years old. I met God in a drunk man lying on the streets of Belfast when I was 12. I met God in the family of a friend who died after a terrible allergic reaction to food. I met God in an orphanage in Tijuana, Mexico, in the lives of children when I was 18. I met God in the slums of India. I met God in the life of a teenage girl who had fallen pregnant and was living in a high-rise flat, alone and frightened, in Birmingham in the early 2000s. I met God in the tears of a Cambodian mother in the Killing Fields. I met God in the frightened eyes of a trafficked young girl in the Midlands of the United Kingdom. I met God in the trembling body of an addict on the streets of Dallas, Texas.

These encounters with the forgotten, the abandoned and the afraid have been moments of encounter and revelation that have shown me that God is not locked in our churches or trapped within our theological ivory towers. God is not concealed behind our theological language and our worship services. Wherever there is brokenness and heartache, God is. This upside-down kingdom flips us out of our comfort and into the pain of the world, where we see God and are met by God in ways that undo us and remake us. These encounters pull away the facades of pietistic protection that we build around ourselves and expose us to the possibility that God is at work in the world, and that it is our task to join God in the divine purpose of transformation until 'the earth will be filled with the knowledge of the glory of the LORD, as the waters cover the sea.'[6]

Everybody matters: churches for all

I first became involved in ministry with people who are disabled in the early 2000s. I had just become the Head of Church, Mission, Evangelism and Prayer at the Evangelical Alliance, and as part of that work I picked up several networks that the Alliance managed or enabled at the time. One of them was a network that brought together Christian charities that worked within the worlds of disability. Groups such as Torch Trust for the blind, Through the Roof, the Shaftesbury Society, Christian Deaf Link UK, Prospects and Livability were working hard both to reach and to release and celebrate people who were disabled. Having had first-hand experience of disability in my own life, I quickly realized that these were my people.

We dreamed and schemed together of how to raise the profile of disabled people in churches, and we devised plans we hoped would ensure that churches were open, welcoming and accessible places for people who lived with disability. In 2004 and 2005, we went on the road with events to help churches address issues of inclusion for disabled people in advance of new UK-wide legislation that would be introduced in 2006. Again and again, we talked about language, posture, buildings, ramps, accessible toilets, fonts for literature, use of British Sign Language, colour differentiation in buildings, working with people who had differing neurological pathways, hidden disabilities such as partial deafness or autism or epilepsy. We cajoled, challenged and pleaded with church leaders to see people who were disabled as equal in value and worth to all others and we reminded them that all are made in God's image,[7] that we are each fearfully and wonderfully made,[8] and that God's house was called to be a like a Great Banquet where 'the poor, the crippled, the blind, and the lame' would be welcomed.[9] Indeed, we wanted churches to understand that without the presence of those living with disability in our communities, our churches themselves would become impoverished and less.

In all the work that we undertook as a collective, we were met with the same two observations again and again. First, church leaders would ask us what they had to do to be 'compliant' with the impending legislation. Second, they would often remark that they had not had much time to get up to speed with the requirements of the law. Both observations caused increasing consternation and disappointment in us as a team. We always felt that the question of compliance was simply a polite way to ascertain what the minimum requirement was, and that the suggestion that churches had not had a lot of time to adapt for disabled people should be met with the wry observation that two thousand years may not have seemed like a long time to them, but it was a very long time!

My interactions with the various charities working in the field of disability for and with the church continue. I count it a privilege to minister with people who are disabled and I thank God for the wonderful insights and perspectives that we can gain from one another.

Watching how these leaders and the agencies they led responded to the widespread apathy of local church leaders opened my eyes to the reality that churches very often forget that everyone matters. In the flipped kingdom, disability is not something that defines someone. Instead, it is so often something that we are *doing* to others. We further disable people who are disabled by our words, our attitudes or our ignorance. This is not so in God's kingdom, where the inherent dignity of people is always to be at the centre of our thinking and our interactions.

We see this inherent valuing of others across the ministry of Jesus. He never sees people as a means to an end; he sees them as people. Where others define someone as a demoniac and force him to live among the dead in a graveyard, Jesus sees a person.[10] Where others ostracize a woman, Jesus drinks water with her.[11] Where others see women as incapable of leadership, Jesus gives them a place at his feet as rabbis in training.[12] Where others tell the blind to shut up, Jesus hears their cry.[13]

My engagement with people who are disabled has left me breathless at their courage and shamefaced at the church's ignorance and prejudice. I think of a woman I know who has fought throughout her ministry to support children with additional needs and their families in the church. As a wheelchair user herself, she has consistently run into ignorance and prejudice, but she battles on, refusing to give up. I think of a couple who are friends of my wife Debbie and me. They lead churches together and are amazing. The husband is blind, and I am constantly humbled at his determination and his commitment. Despite setbacks, obstacles and mistreatment at the hands of God's people, they continue to serve the church and advance the kingdom.

Far too often, our churches have been guilty of preferring the wealthy, the well and the wise. We have blatantly disobeyed the call of James:

> My brothers and sisters, do you with your acts of favouritism really believe in our glorious Lord Jesus Christ? For if a person with gold rings and in fine clothes comes into your assembly, and if a poor person in dirty clothes also comes in, and if you take notice of the one wearing the fine clothes and say, 'Have a seat here, please', while to the one who is poor you say, 'Stand there', or, 'Sit at my feet', have you not made distinctions among yourselves, and become judges with evil thoughts? Listen, my beloved brothers and sisters. Has not God chosen the poor in the world to be rich in faith and to be heirs of the kingdom that he has promised to those who love him? But you have dishonoured the poor. Is it not the rich who oppress you? Is it not they who drag you into court? Is it not they who blaspheme the excellent name that was invoked over you?
> (James 2.1–7)

This is not how it is in the upside-down kingdom. The beautiful presence and ministry of people in the church who are disabled is a reminder to me that, while the world around us and our culture look primarily at the outward appearance, God looks at the heart.[14] From the story of Abel's murder at the hands of his brother, Cain,[15] to the welcoming in of lepers[16] and making way for the paralysed man to get to him,[17] the Bible overflows with stories of people whom others rejected being welcomed into the family of God. Isaac was the weaker one. Jacob was the one of weaker character. David was

15

the youngest. Ruth was not a Hebrew. Rahab was a prostitute. Paul was a murderer.

God delights in welcoming the unexpected, seeing beauty where others see shame. God's people are not so good at seeing past externals, though – despite the call that we should welcome the stranger and make room for the alien.[18] That should not be such a surprise to us, since Christ himself was 'the stone that the builders rejected', yet he has become our chief cornerstone.[19]

The tragedy is that our churches so often treat disabled people in the way that Christ was treated. They saw him as 'a stone that makes them stumble, and a rock that makes them fall'.[20] Instead of welcoming those who are modern-day Mephibosheths and enabling them to sit with us at the king's table,[21] we continue to place shame upon them (the name 'Mephibosheth' means 'dispeller of shame') and force them to live in a place of forgottenness (Lodebar, where Mephibosheth lived, means 'place of forgottenness' or 'place of abandonment').

Instead of being communities of hope, we have too often become communities of hindrance. Instead of opening doors, we have closed them. Instead of displaying the beauty of a diverse body where everyone is included and everyone matters, we have allowed ourselves to be monochrome cut-outs of uniformity. We have too often missed the wild, untamed potential of releasing people into their calling because we have labelled them as disabled and then disabled them with our labels.

The beauty of the kingdom explored through the gospel of Matthew

These are just two examples: the open-armed embrace of James and those involved in serving with and reaching disabled people. They remind us of the beauty and the potential of living out the values of the upside-down kingdom, of letting God flip us into a more biblical, more beautiful and more bountiful way of being. Meeting God in the lives of the poor and excluded, learning to live out of our weaknesses and fragility and remembering that everyone matters in God's kingdom are intrinsically important principles that should undergird our lives together as followers of Christ. Our world is yearning for this kind of community – one where we are all noticed, we all matter and we all belong.

What does it mean to live as kingdom people, though? *Flipped: Life in the Upside-down Kingdom* is my attempt to explore this question with you, and for myself. It is by no means the only way of doing so. Across the church of Jesus Christ in the world, the question of how to live as a kingdom citizen is being explored, explained, unpacked and considered by thousands of people. In articles, books, teaching series and blogs, my fellow believers are trying to think aloud as we attempt to figure this out.[22]

Amid the many ways in which others are exploring this important topic,[23] I want to invite you to consider with me what it means to be flipped and to live in the upside-down kingdom – the kingdom of God – through focusing on one book in the Bible – the gospel according to Matthew. Matthew's gospel presents one of the clearest portrayals of God's kingdom found anywhere in the Bible. It is, in a very real sense, a kingdom gospel. In it we are confronted with a vision of Jesus which positions him as the King of this kingdom in powerful ways and calls all who claim to follow him to live as citizens of the kingdom in our individual lives and in our lives together.

Matthew also draws us into a vision of the world and of the future, where the reign and the rule of the King shape everything. As we encounter this motif across his gospel, we are left speechless by the magnificence of King Jesus, humbled by the realization that we are invited, as Christ's followers, to be citizens of this kingdom, breathless at the breadth and possibilities of kingdom life and hope-laden as we are reminded of the fuller implications of the promises and ultimate purposes of God in establishing his kingdom in the ways that he has.

As we trace the thread of the kingdom through the chapters of Matthew, we will uncover a series of ideas that have the power to change how we see God, ourselves, the church, the world and our place and purpose in it. Think of what we are going to do with Matthew's gospel as an exploration in five parts, each part explored in a chapter of this book, considering together how our views are flipped by the teaching, life, example, commands and promises of Jesus.

In a world that says, 'Be your own king,' we will consider the call of Jesus which flips that by saying, 'I am the King.'

We'll then turn our attention to what it means to have Jesus as our King and how this turns our natural instincts upside down too. As the world tells us to chase popularity, Jesus commands us to welcome everybody.

Our third turn will explore what Matthew tells us is the purpose of the kingdom, and we'll discover another flip in ideas here. In a culture that reassures us with the idea that we should keep all that we can, we'll discover that Jesus calls us to give all that we have.

Having considered the King of the kingdom, the people of the kingdom and the purpose of the kingdom, we'll turn our attention to the perspective that kingdom living provides us and how that also turns us upside down. All around us, our culture creates increasing anxiety and uncertainty as it presents us with reasons to worry about tomorrow, while Jesus tells us to trust God today.

Lastly, we'll turn our attention to the importance of hopefulness and the power of God's promises to us in his kingdom. Whereas the world tells us each to become our own boss and to be in control of our own destinies, Jesus flips this by telling us to become like children.

I will finish each section with a prayer that links to that aspect of God's kingdom for us today. Holy Spirit, we invite you to turn our lives upside down.

Introduction: The 'flipped' foundations

Before we get to chapter 1, I need to set out some broader principles of the kingdom of God in the gospel of Matthew as waypoints for us in the journey that we are going to make. Think of them as navigational aids that will keep us on course as we make our way through the rich, dense material in the gospel that relates to Jesus and the upside-down kingdom. You may be familiar with these ideas, in which case you should feel free to jump to chapter 1 now, but I recommend you don't do that. Instead, take a bit of time to familiarize yourself with the general terrain that we are going to be inhabiting through the rest of *Flipped: Life in the Upside-down Kingdom*. When you know where you are, you know better what to look for. Or, to put it another way, knowing what you need to look out for when you are on a journey means that you are more likely to notice it when it appears.

Matthew's presentation of the kingdom of God is so counter-intuitive that we need to take a moment to catch the bigger picture of it. He doesn't just present a modified version of the way the people of his day understand power and authority; rather, his message turns their thinking on its head at the deepest of levels. His gospel is littered with references to this flipped kingdom in which so much is upside down compared to the culture and expectations that surround him and his peers.

The phrase Matthew most often uses is the 'kingdom of heaven'. He does so because he has his audience in mind, who are mainly Jewish. Their understanding of a king is one who would come, as their deliverer, to dislodge the powerful Roman oppressors and liberate the Jewish people and the land of Israel. Their king will be powerful, triumphant and victorious in all the most traditional of ways. They never imagine a king who will be a servant, or a victory that will look like a defeat. They want a general, not a carpenter! Matthew has a lot of work to do in helping them understand what the kingdom of heaven means.

For devout Jews, phrases such as 'the kingdom' or 'the kingdom of heaven' were synonymous with the rule and reign of God, who was in heaven, which would be demonstrated on the earth. Over time, their use of the phrase 'the kingdom of heaven' became eponymous with God, God's character and God's will. Ultimately, the phrase became interchangeable with the very idea of God. They believed that God wanted to demonstrate the kingdom of heaven fully on the earth. Their deep respect for the divine name meant that they would use such alternative phraseology to avoid being blasphemous and to honour the commandment given to them by Moses, which is often called the third commandment in Christian circles:

> You shall not make wrongful use of the name of the LORD
> your God, for the LORD will not acquit anyone who misuses
> his name.
> (Exodus 20.7)

We need to understand some of the concepts that Matthew uses to portray the kingdom of heaven before we look at the specific implications these have on us.[1] Matthew points to the ultimate sovereignty of God in our world through a very unexpected kingdom. He uses old words in new ways. For him, the kingdom of heaven means the same as the phrase 'the kingdom of God' in the other gospels.[2] I want to explore the meaning of the kingdom, the character of the kingdom, the coming of the kingdom, the demands of the kingdom, the church and the kingdom and the enemy of the kingdom to set out some preliminary ideas about the upside-down kingdom, before exploring the King of the kingdom using a very particular way in which Matthew helps us see Jesus as this king.[3]

But first, what do we mean by the flipped kingdom?

The meaning of the flipped kingdom

Matthew speaks of this kingdom repeatedly. In my reading of his gospel, I have noted references to the king, the kingdom or the king's throne at least 52 times.[4] He presents a picture of God's rule and reign as radically different from anything that we may have known before. In it, God is primarily approached as our Father,[5] forgiveness is the atmosphere in which we live,[6] and we are carried into an unbreakable and transformative relationship of covenant and love.[7] The principles of this kingdom are not revealed to the powerful, the influential or the well placed; rather, they are revealed to the outcast, the humble and the unexpected. Anyone who considers themselves to have made it, by their own perspective, excludes themselves from this kingdom, but those who know they are broken and that they are not enough are invited and welcomed.

> At that time Jesus said, 'I thank you, Father, Lord of heaven and earth, because you have hidden these things from the wise and the intelligent and have revealed them to infants; yes, Father, for such was your gracious will. All things have been handed over to me by my Father; and no one knows the Son except the Father, and no one knows the Father except the Son and anyone to whom the Son chooses to reveal him.
>
> 'Come to me, all you that are weary and are carrying heavy burdens, and I will give you rest. Take my yoke upon you, and learn from me; for I am gentle and humble in heart, and you will find rest for your souls. For my yoke is easy, and my burden is light.'
> (Matthew 11.25–30)

Matthew records that when Jesus' cousin John the Baptist is imprisoned, John sends Jesus a message (presumably because John is having doubts about whether Jesus is really the King of the kingdom, the Messiah and rescuer of Israel and the world). John asks:

> Are you the one who is to come, or are we to wait for another?
> (Matthew 11.3)

Jesus' reply, which he means as evidence of his kingship and confirming his mission, is remarkable:

> Jesus answered them, 'Go and tell John what you hear and see: the blind receive their sight, the lame walk, the lepers are cleansed, the deaf hear, the dead are raised, and the poor have good news brought to them. And blessed is anyone who takes no offence at me.'
> (Matthew 11.4–6)

In other words, the coming of the kingdom is good news for the poor. It is an annunciation of a flipped sense of significance, value and purpose for those who were considered outliers to healthy, holy society in Israel. This is the very reason that Jesus came, and it is rooted in the Jewish understanding of the reign and rule of God as shown in their Messiah and King. It marked his ministry and was a fundamental part of his identity from beginning to end. To see and hear Jesus is to see and hear the King.

Matthew describes the kingdom as already here *in the presence and person of its King*, Jesus:

> From that time Jesus began to proclaim, 'Repent, for the kingdom of heaven has come near.'
> (Matthew 4.17)

Truly I tell you, among those born of women no one has arisen greater than John the Baptist; yet the least in the kingdom of heaven is greater than he. From the days of John the Baptist until now the kingdom of heaven has suffered violence, and the violent take it by force.
(Matthew 11.11–12)

This flipped kingdom, which is radical, shaped by understanding God as our Father, infused with forgiveness, secured in covenant and offered to the poor, the outcast and the forgotten, is not only promised by God through the Scriptures, but also marked and guarded by the Spirit. Matthew, in chapter 12 of his gospel, gives us an account of Jesus being accused of doing the works that he does by the power of Beelzebul. Jesus will not countenance such an accusation from the religious elite of his day and reveals the true source of his kingdom power and authority:

If I cast out demons by Beelzebul, by whom do your own exorcists cast them out? Therefore they will be your judges. But if it is by the Spirit of God that I cast out demons, then the kingdom of God has come to you.
(Matthew 12.27–28)

The kingdom has come, is coming and will come

The cry, 'Your kingdom come. Your will be done, on earth as it is in heaven',[8] is at one and the same time an indication of the present reality of God's kingdom with us and a future promise. These 14 words, repeated by billions of Christians around the world day after day, root us in the very heart of the upside-down kingdom and present us with its conundrum: it is here yet it is still to come. It is now and it is not yet. What does this mean?

In one sense, the upside-down kingdom has always been and will always be. There is no point at which God has vacated the throne. From beginning to end – in fact, from before the beginning and after the end – God will remain sovereign. This eternal rule and reign of God has always been and demands a response from those to whom it has been revealed.

> I am the LORD your God, who brought you out of the land of Egypt, out of the house of slavery; you shall have no other gods before me.
> (Exodus 20.2–3)

> I, I am the LORD,
> and besides me there is no saviour.
> (Isaiah 43.11)

> I am the LORD, and there is no other;
> besides me there is no god.
> I arm you, though you do not know me,
> so that they may know, from the rising of the sun
> and from the west, that there is no one besides me;
> I am the LORD, and there is no other.
> I form light and create darkness,
> I make weal and create woe;
> I the LORD do all these things.
> (Isaiah 45.5–7)

> But the LORD sits enthroned for ever,
> he has established his throne for judgement.
> He judges the world with righteousness;
> he judges the peoples with equity.
> (Psalm 9.7–8)

> The LORD sits enthroned over the flood;
> the LORD sits enthroned as king for ever.
> (Psalm 29.10)

God has taken his place in the divine council.
(Psalm 82.1)

In another sense, however, this rule and reign is directly connected to Christ in the New Testament, which unequivocally states:

He is the image of the invisible God, the firstborn of all creation; for in him all things in heaven and on earth were created, things visible and invisible, whether thrones or dominions or rulers or powers – all things have been created through him and for him. He himself is before all things, and in him all things hold together. He is the head of the body, the church; he is the beginning, the firstborn from the dead, so that he might come to have first place in everything. For in him all the fullness of God was pleased to dwell, and through him God was pleased to reconcile to himself all things, whether on earth or in heaven, by making peace through the blood of his cross.
(Colossians 1.15–20)

This connection between the established rule and reign of God and the ministry and life of Jesus is vitally important for Matthew, and it is of the utmost importance for those of us who are Christians. One of the most important ways in which this is made clear for us is the way in which Matthew uses Daniel's vision, particularly Daniel 7.13–14:

I saw one like a human being
coming with the clouds of heaven.
And he came to the Ancient One
and was presented before him.
To him was given dominion
and glory and kingship,

that all peoples, nations, and languages
should serve him.
His dominion is an everlasting dominion
that shall not pass away,
and his kingship is one
that shall never be destroyed.
(Daniel 7.13–14)

Daniel's presentation of the kingdom is a three-stranded cord of authority, glory and sovereign power. Matthew's gospel presents Jesus as enfleshing these three strands throughout his ministry. In Christ's birth, God's authority is seen in how the Spirit conceives the Son in the womb of the Virgin Mary[9] and the way in which this fulfils the ancient promises of Scripture,[10] God's glory is seen in the worship offered by the Magi,[11] and God's sovereign power is shown in the way angels figure in the story both in the announcement and guidance given to Joseph[12] and in the way in which the Holy Family is protected from the evil intentions of King Herod.[13]

A similar threefold identification of Jesus with the authority, glory and sovereign power of God is seen throughout Matthew's gospel, whether it is Christ's power over illness, demonic power and creation;[14] his glory in the transfiguration;[15] or his authority over the Sabbath,[16] Israel[17] and evil.[18] Matthew consistently presents Jesus and his ministry as bringing together the elements of the eternal kingship presented in Daniel's vision. Ultimately, for Matthew, the final vindication of the kingly rule of God will be seen when Jesus returns and his kingdom is in plain sight for all to see. Christ will come in glory,[19] rule in authority as he separates the sheep from the goats,[20] and demonstrate divine power in his judgements.[21]

This sense of the upside-down kingdom having come in Jesus' ministry while still coming through his ministry and ultimately being fully established and demonstrated through his ministry, as presented in Matthew's gospel, helps us unravel what are sometimes considered difficult passages. The kingdom is an established reality, a current experience and a future promise – it is progressive and established at the same time. That is why we still have struggle, sin and shame to contend with and why we long to see the kingdom come while at the same time we know it is here. It is why, as kingdom people, we cry, 'Your kingdom come!'

When Jesus challenges his followers to take up their cross and follow him, he links his glory with his authority,[22] then tells them that some present will not die before they see his glory:

> For the Son of Man is to come with his angels in the glory of his Father, and then he will repay everyone for what has been done. Truly I tell you, there are some standing here who will not taste death before they see the Son of Man coming in his kingdom.
> (Matthew 16.27–28)

Is this a mistake made by Jesus, since the disciples did die before they saw the ultimate fulfilment of these words? Not at all, because the very next part of Jesus' ministry that Matthew describes is the transfiguration – a moment when Christ's glory and the glory of the kingdom was revealed:

> Six days later, Jesus took with him Peter and James and his brother John and led them up a high mountain, by themselves. And he was transfigured before them, and his face shone like the sun, and his clothes became dazzling white. Suddenly there appeared to them Moses and Elijah, talking with him . . . suddenly a bright cloud overshadowed them, and from the cloud a voice said, 'This is my Son, the Beloved; with whom I am well pleased; listen to him!'
> (Matthew 17.1–3, 5)

The kingdom that has come, is coming and will come is tied up in this remarkable moment, and when we understand that, so much of our puzzlement over passages like this is resolved.

The same thing happens when Jesus speaks to his disciples about coming persecutions in the destruction of Jerusalem as an act of divine judgement, which would take place in AD 70,[23] and when Jesus speaks to the high priest of his return at the end of time.[24]

Matthew makes it clear that the kingdom will continue to grow, not only in and through the ministry of Jesus himself, but also through the ministry of Jesus as it is lived out in the lives of his disciples. The parables of Jesus, set out by Matthew in chapters 13, 18, 19, 20 and 21, all explain this principle. What is small will grow. What is hidden will be seen. What appears insignificant will become profoundly influential. What is considered worthless is to be prized above everything. What is prized above all else is to be guarded and held securely. The advance of the kingdom is unstoppable. It will infuse the lives of all who are part of it and in turn will infuse the world of which they are part. This great purpose will be fully and finally complete when Christ returns. The seed he plants in his life, death and resurrection will come into full blossom when he breaks the clouds to return.[25] It is in his authority and with his presence that we advance his kingdom:

All authority in heaven and on earth has been given to me. Go therefore and make disciples of all nations, baptizing them in the name of the Father and of the Son and of the Holy Spirit, and teaching them to obey everything that I have commanded you. And remember, I am with you always, to the end of the age. (Matthew 28.18–20)

Kingdom demands

Matthew makes two demands of us in relation to the upside-down kingdom. The first is that we must put it first:

But strive first for the kingdom of God and his righteousness, and all these things will be given to you as well.
(Matthew 6.33)

Enter through the narrow gate; for the gate is wide and the road is easy that leads to destruction, and there are many who take it.
(Matthew 7.13)

Not everyone who says to me, 'Lord, Lord', will enter the kingdom of heaven, but only one who does the will of my Father in heaven.
(Matthew 7.21)

The only way we can do this is by being in a direct and living relationship with the King – Jesus himself. It is only as we make this connection that we can make sense of how we relate to the reign and rule of God. It is as we come to Jesus that we find the kingdom. Jesus does not invite us to come any other way. His invitation is:

Come to me, all you that are weary and are carrying heavy burdens, and I will give you rest.
(Matthew 11.28)

The broken patterns of kingship and obedience found in the story of Israel, with its imperfect kings and its own disobedience as a nation, are transformed in Jesus. He embodies both perfect kingship *and* perfect citizenship:

King and servant met in his person. Jesus is thus both the founder and the embodiment of the kingdom. He is the kingdom in himself. That is why he can call people to himself when he invites them into the kingdom of God.[26]

29

The method of entry into the upside-down kingdom is twofold: repentance and faith. That is why Jesus calls people to repentance and welcomes their repentance at one and the same time.[27]

Once we have entered the kingdom, we are presented with its second demand: changed behaviour. Matthew reminds us that we are to be sheep, not wolves; wheat, not weeds; sheep, not goats; good trees, not bad ones.[28] As we will see later, this is powerfully set out in the Sermon on the Mount,[29] which challenges the priorities, perspectives and practices of those who claim to be kingdom citizens. In short, kingdom citizens have gained the privilege of their citizenship through Christ, and as his citizens we are called to emulate his character and follow in his steps.

The church and the kingdom

Writing in 1894, Washington Gladden noted that the church and the kingdom are not synonymous:

> What is the relation of the church to the kingdom of God? The terms are often used interchangeably; and it is sometimes assumed that the church is simply the kingdom in its organised form. I do not think that this is the true conception. The kingdom of God is the larger; the kingdom includes the church but the church does not include the kingdom.[30]

There is no clearer evidence of this than Jesus' use of the words we translate as 'church' and 'kingdom'. Jesus uses the word for 'church' twice,[31] but the word for kingdom is used more than a hundred times, 53 of them in the gospel of Matthew.[32] The words are most decisively not synonymous. If they were, we should be able to use them interchangeably in the texts where one or the other of them is used. Trying to do that immediately shows us that it does not work. Christ's use of kingdom language is abundant! It is his most used, most emphasized and most descriptive name for the community of God. Only one conclusion can be drawn from this: 'the church must be construed through the kingdom, and not the kingdom through the church'.[33]

Matthew shows us a Jesus who sees himself as the King of this kingdom. The idea of the kingdom is of primary significance and gives definition to the meaning and purpose of the church. Jesus promises to build *his* church,[34] but his definition of this community is one that points to the kingdom of God, not to structures and organization. It is the kingdom of heaven that Jesus announces at the beginning of his ministry:

> From that time Jesus began to proclaim, 'Repent, for the kingdom of heaven has come near.'
> . . . Jesus went throughout Galilee, teaching in their synagogues and proclaiming the good news of the kingdom and curing every disease and every sickness among the people.
> (Matthew 4.17, 23)

His gospel is a gospel 'of the kingdom'.[35] The seed that he sows is the Word,[36] which he describes using several different phrases. It is 'of heaven'[37] and not of 'the kingdoms of this world'. Jesus describes this kingdom seed as 'of God'[38] and not of the kingdom of satan.[39] He also describes it as a kingdom of the truth where he himself embodies that truth and those who are his people are citizens of the King – committed to truth.

> Jesus answered, 'My kingdom is not from this world. If my kingdom were from this world, my followers would be fighting to keep me from being handed over to the Jews. But as it is, my kingdom is not from here.' Pilate asked him, 'So you are a king?' Jesus answered, 'You say that I am a king. For this I was born, and for this I came into the world, to testify to the truth. Everyone who belongs to the truth listens to my voice.' Pilate asked him, 'What is truth?'
> (John 18.36–38)

For Jesus, the kingdom is present,[40] people may enter it,[41] and may even be within it.[42] The kingdom that the church is called to demonstrate is an ethical one; its citizens seek the righteousness of God and pray for its coming by asking that the will of God be done on earth as in heaven.

> Its signs are all spiritual and ethical, relate to gracious helpfulness and service, never to officers or acts of ceremonial. It is universal, open to all without respect to place or race . . . the emphasis falls, not upon officials . . . or on Sacramental acts . . . but upon the people, upon persons, their personal qualities, conduct, character, their state and living before God, their behaviour and ministry amongst men (*sic*). He, indeed, calls disciples and commissions apostles, but he deals with them as men (*sic*) who must be of a given spirit if they would enter the kingdom; their eminence in it depends, not on office, but on spiritual qualities; and their reward, not on dignities possessed, but on the range and kind of service – none being sacerdotal, all spiritual and human.[43]

In short, the church is an embassy of the kingdom, and the kingdom is built on the person, character, work and example of the King. Michael Green describes the church as 'the first instalment of the coming kingdom' and suggests that it is intended 'by its message and way of life to be a colony of heaven'.[44]

We must be careful not to fall into the trap of creating a kingdom theology which applies everything that is said about the kingdom uncritically to the church. When Jesus tells Peter and the disciples that he will build his church, for example, he explains to them that he will do so by giving them the keys of the kingdom.

> And I tell you, you are Peter, and on this rock I will build my church, and the gates of Hades will not prevail against it.

> I will give you the keys of the kingdom of heaven, and what-
> ever you bind on earth will be bound in heaven, and whatever
> you loose on earth will be loosed in heaven.
> (Matthew 16.18–19)

Matthew gives us a Jesus who presents the church as the net, the harvest field, the community on earth that contains both sheep and goats. God will sort out the genuine from the false in the Judgement. The church *should* be the community where the rule and reign of God is seen and experienced – this is our calling, but we are not a pure people. There are people 'in' the church who are not genuinely 'in' the kingdom and do not trust the King;[45] there are people 'within' the church who lead people astray because they are not 'within' the kingdom or obedient to the King;[46] and there are those whose allegiance to the King is shallow and will not endure persecution and challenge,[47] or who will be lured from the King by wealth, comfort and ease.[48]

> No, the church cannot be identified with the kingdom, but
> it does represent that part of God's kingly rule which is no
> longer in open revolt again the rightful king but professes to
> have surrendered to him. And it is the job of the church to
> evangelize, so that the kingdom of God will be spread as other
> rebel subjects come to accept the gracious armistice offered by
> the King.[49]

The enemy of the kingdom

Matthew's gospel presents us with a clear enemy of Christ and his kingly rule – a usurper who wants to dethrone or derail the King and his kingdom. He is the accuser, the liar, the deceiver – satan. This figure is utterly against the kingdom of God and all that it represents. Jesus instructs his followers to pray, 'And do not bring us to the time of trial, but rescue us from the evil one.'[50] The Pharisees accuse Jesus of bringing his kingdom by the power of this figure who has many names, including Beelzebul (which means 'lord of the flies').[51] Using a parable of weeds, Christ makes it perfectly clear that while he, the Son of Man, sows the good seed of 'the children of the kingdom', the weeds are the children 'of the evil one, and the enemy who sowed them is the devil'.[52]

It is satan that tries to tempt Christ away from his mission;[53] who is perceived as 'the strong man' (although Christ is stronger),[54] and it is satan that Jesus names as being the power behind Peter's attempts to stop Jesus going to the cross.[55] It is satan that inspires the crowds[56] and the leaders[57] to oppose Jesus. There is no doubt that the wider gospel story makes it clear that satan is a defeated foe, overthrown by the life and ministry of Jesus – indeed, this is one of the core purposes in the coming of Christ:

> The Son of God was revealed for this purpose, to destroy the works of the devil.
> (1 John 3.8)

> Since, therefore, the children share flesh and blood, he himself likewise shared the same things, so that through death he might destroy the one who has the power of death, that is, the devil, and free those who all their lives were held in slavery by the fear of death.
> (Hebrews 2.14–15)

We should make no mistake about it, however, that satan will appear as appealing and beautiful if it means he can distract us from the purposes of God. King Jesus was alert to his schemes, and so must we be,[58] by recognizing that he comes as an angel of light,[59] or that he tries to convince us that he is nothing more than an idea. His tactics are working. So often, the modern church fails to see this enemy, and as a result we can fall into the trap of making people our enemies instead. If we do not see him as present, we will not arm ourselves to face him. C. S. Lewis saw this tactic and named it in several of his books,[60] including his powerful book, *The Screwtape Letters*:

> If once we can produce our perfect work – the Materialist Magician, the man, not using, but veritably worshipping what he vaguely calls 'Forces', while denying the existence of 'spirits' – then the end of the war will be in sight . . .
>
> I do not think you will have much difficulty in keeping your patient in the dark. The fact that 'devils' are predominantly comic figures in the modern imagination will help you. If any faint suspicion of your existence begins to arise in his mind, suggest to him a picture of something in red tights, and persuade him that since he cannot believe in that (it is an old textbook method of confusing them) he therefore cannot believe in you.[61]

R. C. Sproul recounts that he once asked about 30 college students if they believed in God. Most did, but when he asked if they believed in the devil, only a few raised their hands. He encountered the common objection that is often put today by those who deny the existence of a personal force of evil:

> How can any intelligent person believe in the devil in this day and age? The devil belongs to superstition along with ghosts, goblins and things that go bump in the night.[62]

Such an argument is in direct antithesis to the way in which Matthew tells the story of Jesus. Any examination of Matthew's understanding of the upside-down kingdom would be deficient if it did not acknowledge his very clear belief in, and portrayal of, an enemy of the kingdom. In an age that dismisses such notions as old-fashioned and irrelevant, we would do well to remember the warning of Peter to his readers:

> Humble yourselves therefore under the mighty hand of God, so that he may exalt you in due time. Cast all your anxiety on him, because he cares for you. Discipline yourselves; keep alert. Like a roaring lion your adversary the devil prowls around, looking for someone to devour. Resist him, steadfast in your faith, for you know that your brothers and sisters throughout the world are undergoing the same kinds of suffering.
> (1 Peter 5.6–9)

Step back

The church auditorium was buzzing with expectation and excitement. It was about 6 p.m. The music group had finished its practice and people were milling around. Some were drinking coffee, some were chatting to friends and some were making their way to a seat. Our building at Gold Hill Baptist Church was old and awkward, but we loved it. So many lives had been changed through encounters with God in this space. Tonight, I prayed, would be no different. I was so excited about what the Lord would do.

It was around 2014 and we were experiencing a new sense of the Holy Spirit's presence in our gatherings. We had changed the focus of our Sunday evening gatherings so that they were more relaxed, and they had become a space where most of the people attending came with an expectation that they would meet, and be transformed by, the power of the Holy Spirit. We continued to be committed to preaching the good news of the forgiveness of sins and to giving people an opportunity to respond to God, but there was a new and vibrant sense of expectation in the air. We had changed the name of the gatherings to 'Fresh' and there was certainly a fresh bounce in everyone's step.

That evening was also a baptismal service. A few people had recently become Christians, and we were looking forward to hearing their stories and celebrating their public declarations of their commitment to Christ. A number of those being baptized were young people – in their mid- to late teens. As I stood on the platform, I was looking through their baptismal verses. My friend and colleague, James, had been praying about verses for the candidates. We would share one with each of them before baptizing them and praying for them. I couldn't wait.

Then, at around 6.25 p.m., just a few minutes before the service began, the doors at the back of the auditorium opened and around 35 young people burst into the meeting. They had come from our youth service. We had started it a few months before and it was amazing. Our young people were growing in faith, and they were so on fire for God! I don't think I have ever seen such an exciting thing happening in a local church youth group. We couldn't keep them from church! On Sundays, they would meet at 10 a.m., then hang out together, then have their youth meeting (it was called 'Breathe') and then they would walk up through the village together to get to the 6.30 p.m. meeting. They were alive, alert and attuned to the Holy Spirit. Their presence in our meetings was nothing short of electrifying. They would sit at the front, passionate in their worship, open in their hearts and attentive to what God wanted to say. They changed the atmosphere in the whole fellowship. That night, after we had finished the service, they gathered round their friends who had been baptized to pray for them. They were laying hands on them, prophesying over them, hugging them. It was a beautiful thing. This was what God's flipped kingdom looked like, and I loved it.

I paint that little cameo so that you can see all the rather complex ideas of Matthew's portrayal of the kingdom in a simple scene. This picture shows the meaning of the kingdom – it is a reality that you can be part of whatever your age, whatever your background and whatever people think about you. You could see the character of the kingdom in the excitement, anticipation and straightforward faith of these young people. They weren't theologically trained. They didn't have all the answers. They certainly were not perfect. But they were open, hungry and childlike.

I saw in that season what the coming of the kingdom looks like. Small seeds planted in the lives of ordinary young people and families; the faith of one impacting the life of another; the touch of God in one area of the community spilling over into the wider community; a middle-class church being turned upside down by the passion of a bunch of teenagers. The whole church – in fact, the whole community – was being changed by what God was doing in the lives of these young people. I loved Gold Hill, and one of the many reasons that I loved them (and still do) was that from the oldest to the youngest, from the most reserved to the most progressive, this community (or most of them – more on that in a moment) really loved these young people and we were willing to learn from them. The kingdom seed in their lives was impacting us all.

You can also see the demands of the kingdom in my story because these young people were not compromising. They were unequivocally committed to God's purposes and kingdom. From that small group we saw engineers, lawyers, doctors, pastors, worship leaders, businesswomen and men, church planters and all kinds of other vocations stirred and released. They were laying their lives open to God and living in holiness and obedience, and their radical commitment was challenging everyone else in the church. And we see in this picture the relationship between the church and the kingdom because, while these young people were falling in love with the church, they refused to be defined by it because they wanted to be defined by God's kingdom and purposes. They weren't being changed by the church; they were being changed by God. They weren't hungry to be Baptists; they were hungry to be followers of Christ and his kingdom! Their priorities and commitment were not simply present in the church; God was changing the church through them. He was using the least, the youngest and the most inexperienced to breathe fresh passion into the older, more-established and more-set-in-their-ways members of the community. They really were like a breath of fresh air.

Sadly, the work of the enemy of the kingdom could also be seen. Some people felt threatened enough to begin to criticize the youth congregation. Some of my fellow leaders started to try to control what the Holy Spirit was doing and to put limits on where he might go. A small group of people who felt that our Sunday evenings were becoming too shaped by this wider move of the Spirit began to argue that things should be changed. So the timing of the meeting shifted, and the young people stopped walking up the hill to get there in time. We lost their energy, their passion, their raw love of God. Then the way the youth congregation itself met was changed, and the young people started to get managed. In the end, this move of God was halted because we got in the way of what God wanted to do for the kingdom. God still did amazing things, but I think that God wanted to do more for the kingdom in that season, and we stopped him doing it.

Matthew's traits of the kingdom – its character, its coming, its demands, its tensions with the church, and ultimately its enemy – were all seen in that season. It wasn't just other people who stopped what God wanted. I stopped it too. I did so because I allowed the wrong people to have the loudest voices. I should have remembered that the voice that mattered more than anyone else's was the voice of Jesus – the King of the kingdom.

It is to that very idea of Jesus as our King that we now turn. This is not merely a theoretical concept to ponder or a theological muse to entertain us. It raises profoundly important issues that followers of Jesus must wrestle with if we are to live faithfully and fruitfully for him.

What does it mean, for you or for me, to describe Jesus as the King?

1

King of the kingdom

The world says, 'Be your own king.'
Jesus says, 'I am the King.'

Render therefore unto Caesar the things which are Caesar's;
and unto God the things that are God's.
(Matthew 22.21, KJV)

But they cried out, 'Away with Him, away with Him! Crucify
Him!'
 Pilate said to them, 'Shall I crucify your King?'
 The chief priests answered, 'We have no king but Caesar!'
(John 19.15, NKJV)

Jesus did not come to offer the world a sin-management system
(although in his coming he deals with our sin and separation from
God once and for all). He did not come simply to ensure that we go
to heaven when we die (although his coming ensures that when we
die, we go to be with Christ and will never be separated from God).
He did not enter time and history to sort out a moral and spiritual
mess that took God by surprise (although his coming deals with our
moral failures, our spiritual brokenness and our self-centredness,
arrogance and pride). Jesus did not come to establish a religion
(although in his coming are the seeds of hope for his people – both
believing Israel and the Gentile church, who are made one new
humanity by his grace).

 In his coming, Jesus Christ announces the rule and reign of God.
He comes as the King of all kings and the Lord of all lords. His

coming is an annunciation of the eternal and unbreakable power of Almighty God over all created things. His coming is a declaration of sovereignty. His coming is a decisive moment in the divine plan when God's reign and rule, established before time itself began, is powerfully and personally displayed in the life of one man, who is both fully God and fully human. The birth, life, death, resurrection, ascension, heavenly intercession and the promised physical, visible and triumphant return of Jesus Christ to earth to rule and reign are all vitally important. The ultimate seat of authority is occupied – God is on the throne. Jesus is King. Seeing this, living in this, being captivated by this, changes everything.

His reign, however, is not like the reign of an earthly monarch or an elected president. His principles, priorities and practices turn everything upside down. The poor are given a special place in his kingdom. The broken are welcomed. The lost are found. The forgotten are not only noticed, but they are also vitally important. His reign and rule are not with a fist of iron, but with the powerful touch of grace.

Archbishop Desmond Tutu (1931–2021) was the spiritual leader of South Africa through some of its darkest and most troubled years. He was convinced that Jesus Christ was King. That conviction led him to challenge violence, to confront racism, to stand with the downtrodden and overlooked and to campaign tirelessly for a world where the rule and the reign of God would be more evidenced in how women and men saw and treated each other. His powerful prayer, 'Victory Is Ours', was rooted in his belief in the absolute rule and reign of God through the Lord Jesus Christ. The poem, which many of you will be familiar with, speaks of goodness triumphing over evil and love over hate, and says that light is strong enough to overcome the darkness, that victory can be ours through God's great love.[1]

Tutu was profoundly impacted by the actions of Trevor Huddleston, who became the Anglican Archbishop of Cape Town.

Earlier in his ministry, Huddleston, who was also convinced of the kingship of Jesus, had raised his hat to a Black woman seated on a bus. This was a revolutionary, countercultural act in a society that saw Black people as underlings and inferior to White people. The woman to whom Huddleston raised his hat was Desmond Tutu's mother, and the act of defiance by Huddleston, which carried with it an inherent recognition of Tutu's mother and all people who were Black, had a lifelong impact on Tutu.[2] Huddleston's stance against the apartheid system was rooted in his conviction of the lordship of Christ and the subsequent message of hope and liberation it carried to all people.[3]

Commenting on how we read the gospels today and their impact on our lives, Tom Wright expresses a deep yearning for rediscovery of the kingship of Christ:

> Can we learn to read the gospels better, more in tune with what their original writers intended . . . Can we discover, by doing this, a new vision for God's mission in the world, in and through Jesus, and then – now! – in and through his followers? And, in doing so, can we grow closer together in mission and life, in faith and hope, and even in love? Might a fresh reading of the gospels, in other words, clear the way for renewed efforts in mission and unity? Is that what it would look like if we really believed that the living god was king on earth as in heaven?
>
> That, after all, is the story all four gospels tell . . . of how God became king.[4]

As we consider the King of this kingdom, we must remember that all the traits and characteristics we see in the King ought to automatically be present in the kingdom over which he reigns and rules. It was the traits of the King that shaped Desmond Tutu's understanding of his own life and ministry. Tutu never forgot this reality. It infused everything he said and did in his ministry. He wrote:

> God showed himself there as a saving God, as a doing, an active kind of God . . . and he showed himself to be a God of liberation, the great Exodus God, who took the side of the oppressed, the exploited ones, the downtrodden, the marginalised ones. He was no fence sitter. He took sides against the powerful on behalf of the widow, the orphan and the alien – classes of people who were often at the back of the queue, at the bottom of the pile . . . the theme of setting free, of rescuing captives or those who have been kidnapped, is one that runs through the Bible as the golden thread.[5]

It was because he was convinced of the kingship of Jesus that Desmond Tutu could face any person in power. He knew that his Sovereign sat on a throne that no one could take away.

This deep-seated conviction pervades the gospels, nowhere more than the gospel of Matthew. The character of the King changes everything for the way we understand what it means to be followers of Christ today. One of the core ways in which Matthew sets this out to us is by portraying Jesus as a new Moses.

King Jesus – the new Moses

Apart from Abraham, the father of Judaism, Moses is the most central human figure in Jewish thinking and theology. He is the great deliverer of Israel in the exodus; the one to whom the law is entrusted for the covenant community; the prophet who speaks out the will and purpose of God to God's people. He stands in the roles of both priest and apostle as he pleads with God for Israel and pleads with Israel to follow God and leads them into new territory; and he is a king to Israel before the formal appointment of

43

kings.[6] References to his kingly role are peppered across the Old Testament,[7] with two of the most powerful images of this aspect of his ministry found in a short phrase in the first section of the book of Exodus and at the end of Deuteronomy respectively:

> . . . and Moses carried the staff of God in his hand.
> (Exodus 4.20)

> Moses charged us with the law,
> as a possession for the assembly of Jacob.
> There arose a king in Jeshurun,
> when the leaders of the people assembled –
> the united tribes of Israel.
> (Deuteronomy 33.4–5)

In the words from Exodus, this 'staff' and the words used to describe it are identified as the sceptre[8] of kingly authority in other parts of the Old Testament.[9] Deuteronomy is the only place where Moses is named king.

Moses himself pointed to the future and announced:

> The LORD your God will raise up for you a prophet like me from among your own people; you shall heed such a prophet.
> (Deuteronomy 18.15)

For many, this promise of a 'prophet like me' not only pointed to the prophetic ministries and reigns of Joshua and Samuel and those who flowed from them, but also to David and other prophet-kings, and ultimately to one great Prophet–Priest–King who would not only carry the mantle of Moses, but go further.[10] Matthew's portrayal of Jesus as a new Moses, written as it is for a mostly Jewish audience, points clearly and unequivocally to Christ as the wearer of this mantle – the new King whose reign and rule will somehow fulfil all of the elements of Moses' ministry as deliverer, law-bringer, prophet, priest, apostle and king.

What the gospel of Matthew says about Jesus as King in the upside-down kingdom.

The opening words of Matthew, and therefore of the whole of the New Testament, point us to the unique ministry and identity of Jesus Christ:

> An account of the genealogy of Jesus the Messiah, the son of David, the son of Abraham.
> (Matthew 1.1)

In one short sentence, Matthew establishes the Davidic and royal identity of Jesus as well as his Abrahamic and Jewish centrality, and in so doing places him at the very centre of God's purposes for God's people and for the world. In his opening words, Matthew unfolds the legal ancestry and spiritual line of Mary's Son and establishes his legitimacy as the rightful messianic heir. As he interweaves the role and place of the Holy Spirit in the virginal conception and birth of Jesus, he also points to Christ's divine Sonship. In just a few sentences, Matthew's gospel explodes with the announcement of the Saviour, the Messiah, the Son of David and the heir of Abraham. In Jesus we see the embodiment of Israel, with all her calling, her hopes and her covenant.

This in itself is breathtaking, but Matthew goes further. The details he includes in his gospel, the way in which he presents Jesus and the very structure of his gospel present Jesus as a new Moses, the rightful King of the kingdom.[11] By combining these elements – Moses, Abraham, David and the promised Messiah – Matthew leaves his readers in no doubt that, in Jesus, the 'hopes and fears of all the years' are met.[12]

1 The birth narratives: just like Moses, the baby Jesus is pursued by an evil king

There are marked similarities between the birth stories of Moses in the book of Exodus and the way in which Matthew portrays Jesus' birth. These begin with the command of Pharaoh to kill all the baby boys in Israel in an attempt to limit the power of the Hebrew people, and Herod's command to kill all the infant boys in Jerusalem in an attempt to kill the child to whom the wise men had come to pay homage.

> Then Pharaoh commanded all his people, 'Every boy that is born to the Hebrews you shall throw into the Nile, but you shall let every girl live.'
> (Exodus 1.22)

> When Herod realised that he had been outwitted by the Magi, he was furious, and he gave orders to kill all the boys in Bethlehem and its vicinity who were two years old and under, in accordance with the time he had learned from the Magi.
> (Matthew 2.16, NIV UK)

Just as Moses is saved by being hidden in a basket and cast onto the great River Nile, where he is found by the daughter of Pharaoh and cared for,[13] so Jesus is saved by being brought to Egypt by Joseph and Mary.[14] The rescue of Moses is to be assumed as a miraculous intervention of God because the basket he is in comes to Pharaoh's daughter. The rescue of Jesus is clearly described in miraculous language because the Lord specifically appears to Joseph in a dream to instruct him:

> An angel of the Lord appeared to Joseph in a dream and said, 'Get up, take the child and his mother, and flee to Egypt, and

remain there until I tell you; for Herod is about to search for the child, to destroy him.'
(Matthew 2.13)

The rooting of the birth story of Jesus in Egypt itself[15] is a bold, clear and unavoidable identification of Jesus with Moses for Matthew's original hearers. The parallel lines of the stories of Jesus and Moses are woven across Matthew's narratives like threads of meaning for any Jewish hearer. When Moses faces danger because of his violence against another Hebrew, he flees Pharaoh and Egypt for Israel[16] and then returns to Egypt from Israel forty years later.[17] Jesus' journey is the reverse of this – Joseph takes him from Israel to Egypt and then back again.[18]

And so begins a weaving of the story of Moses and the story of Jesus that works across Matthew's gospel – but always portraying Jesus as a greater Moses. For Matthew, Moses is the one who points to Jesus, not the other way round. Moses may have become a king-like figure for a while, but Matthew is very clear that Jesus was born as King. Matthew announces Jesus' kingship not as an event in the future, but as a reality from the moment of his conception and birth. There may have been a pretender on the throne (Herod) at the time of Jesus' birth, but Jesus is (as far as I know) the only person ever born as King. He did not inherit the title or the role – he was born as King.

In the time of King Herod, after Jesus was born in Bethlehem of Judea, wise men from the East came to Jerusalem, asking, *'Where is the child who has been born king of the Jews? For we observed his star at its rising, and have come to pay him homage.'*
(Matthew 2.1–2, emphasis mine)

2 Moses, Jesus and mountains

Moses meets God on a mountain, where he receives instructions from God on how God's people are to live. Mountains in the life of Moses are places of encounter, revelation and empowerment right until the end of his days.[19]

> Then Moses went up to God; the LORD called to him from the mountain . . .
> (Exodus 19.3)

> Then Moses and Aaron, Nadab and Abihu, and seventy of the elders of Israel went up, and they saw the God of Israel.
> (Exodus 24.9–10)

> The LORD said to Moses, 'Come up to me on the mountain, and wait there; and I will give you the tablets of stone, with the law and the commandment, which I have written for their instruction.' So Moses set out with his assistant Joshua, and Moses went up into the mountain of God . . .
> Then Moses went up on the mountain, and the cloud covered the mountain. The glory of the LORD settled on Mount Sinai, and the cloud covered it for six days; on the seventh day he called to Moses out of the cloud. Now the appearance of the glory of the LORD was like a devouring fire on the top of the mountain in the sight of the people of Israel. Moses entered the cloud, and went up on the mountain. Moses was on the mountain for forty days and forty nights.
> (Exodus 24.12–13, 15–18)

Matthew echoes this place of encounter in the way he describes Jesus' ministry – not once but several times. It is on a mountain that the devil brings Jesus his third temptation.[20] Matthew frames the teaching of Jesus with mountains; indeed, that is why it is known as the Sermon on the Mount:

> When Jesus saw the crowds, he went up the mountain; and after he sat down, his disciples came to him. Then he began to speak, and taught them, saying . . .
> (Matthew 5.1–2)

> When Jesus had come down from the mountain, great crowds followed him.
> (Matthew 8.1)

Jesus goes up on a mountainside to pray,[21] and he is on a mountain when he feeds the four thousand.[22] He is also on a mountain when he is transfigured before Peter, James and John, where they see him in conversation with Elijah and . . . *Moses*!

> Six days later, Jesus took with him Peter and James and his brother John and led them up a high mountain, by themselves.
> (Matthew 17.1)

When Moses met with God on the mountain, his face shone, but when Jesus was transfigured, his whole body shone, and both Elijah and Moses were in places of homage and humility to Jesus:

> Moses came down from Mount Sinai. As he came down from the mountain with the two tablets of covenant in his hand, Moses did not know that the skin of his face shone because he had been talking with God. When Aaron and all the Israelites saw Moses, the skin of his face was shining, and they were afraid to come near him.
> (Exodus 34.29–30)

> And he was transfigured before them, and his face shone like
> the sun, and his clothes became dazzling white. Suddenly
> there appeared to them Moses and Elijah, talking with him.
> (Matthew 17.2–3)

As Jesus prepares his disciples for his departure and warns them of
what is to come, he does so on the Mount of Olives.[23] And it is on
a mountain that Jesus gives his disciples the Great Commission:

> Now the eleven disciples went to Galilee, to the mountain
> to which Jesus had directed them. When they saw him, they
> worshipped him; but some doubted. And Jesus came and said
> to them, 'All authority in heaven and on earth has been given
> to me. Go therefore and make disciples of all nations, baptiz-
> ing them in the name of the Father and of the Son and of the
> Holy Spirit, and teaching them to obey everything that I have
> commanded you. And remember, I am with you always, to the
> end of the age.
> (Matthew 28.16–20)

These parallels are remarkable, and their inference is unmissable.
Matthew invites his hearers to follow Jesus as he climbs mountains
of temptation, instruction, the miraculous, transfiguration, eschato-
logical consummation and commission. On each occasion, we are
reminded that Jesus is a New Moses – one who reigns and rules as
King of the kingdom.

But perhaps the most powerful mountain of all in the gospel of
Matthew is the mountain of the crucifixion – Golgotha. Not named
as a mountain in Matthew but known as one nevertheless, and the
place at which Christ is lifted high above the earth:

> And when they came to a place called Golgotha (which means
> Place of a Skull), they offered him wine to drink, mixed with

gall; but when he tasted it, he would not drink it. And when they had crucified him, they divided his clothes among themselves by casting lots; then they sat down there and kept watch over him. Over his head they put the charge against him, which read, 'This is Jesus, the King of the Jews.'
(Matthew 27.33–37)

3 Moses, Jesus and blood

For the Jews, Moses was the Great Deliverer, the one who had been raised up by God to set them free from the tyranny and oppression of the Egyptians. Deeply rooted within the Jewish psyche was the expectation that God would send them a great deliverer. In their history, the depiction of Moses as the one who led them out of Egypt and into the promised land was the singularly most important image of their deliverance. This account of God's liberation through Moses became an important reminder that God would deliver them again, and sits at the heart of the writing of the letter to the Hebrews in the New Testament. It also shaped the central understanding that God would send them a new deliverer in the form of their Messiah. Central to this great deliverance (or *exodus*) was the way in which God promised to protect the Hebrew people. Moses became the mediator of this covenant through the shedding of the blood of the Passover lamb and its sprinkling on the doorposts of the Hebrew homes.[24]

Moses took the blood and dashed it on the people, and said, 'See the blood of the covenant that the LORD has made with you in accordance with all these words.'
(Exodus 24.8)

Matthew presents us with Jesus instigating a new covenant, of which he is both the mediator and the sacrifice:

> While they were eating, Jesus took a loaf of bread, and after blessing it he broke it, gave it to the disciples, and said, 'Take, eat; this is my body.' Then he took a cup, and after giving thanks he gave it to them, saying, 'Drink from it, all of you; for this is my blood of the covenant, which is poured out for many for the forgiveness of sins.'
> (Matthew 26.26–28)

4 Moses, Jesus and forty days

As Moses met with God on Mount Sinai, we discover that he remained there for forty days and forty nights, in which time he 'neither ate bread nor drank water'.[25] Similarly, Matthew tells us that Jesus fasted for forty days after his baptism and before the beginning of his ministry in Galilee:

> Then Jesus was led up by the Spirit into the wilderness to be tempted by the devil. He fasted for forty days and forty nights, and afterwards he was famished.
> (Matthew 4.1–2)

5 Moses, Jesus and commissioning[26]

As Moses' time of death approached, we are told that God involved him in the commissioning of Joshua.[27] This commissioning involved Joshua being told that he would lead the people of Israel into a foreign land, that he was to observe all that God had commanded the people to do, through Moses,[28] and that God's presence would remain with him and with the people of Israel.[29] Similarly Jesus, Matthew's new Moses, commissions his people to obey God's law, to extend God's kingdom into the whole earth and to obey God's commands; and Jesus promises never to leave them as they take up this Great Commission.[30]

6 Moses' death and Jesus' death

Jewish tradition believes that at the death of Moses, 'the angels mourned, the heavens were shaken, lightnings flashed, and a heavenly voice spoke'.[31] Scripture seems to suggest that God personally buried Moses and that no one knows his place of rest.[32] Matthew details many strange occurrences that were also present at the death of the Lord Jesus. At Christ's death, the sun goes dark,[33] the veil of the temple is ripped in two from the top to the bottom,[34] the earth shakes[35] and the dead rise from their graves.[36]

7 Moses and the Pentateuch: Jesus and the discourses

Jewish and Christian scholarship has traditionally attributed the first five books of the Bible, known as the Pentateuch, to the authorship of Moses. Whoever may have written the first five books of the Bible, they are deeply connected to the story of Moses. Matthew, in his positioning of Jesus as the new Moses, constructs his gospel around five major discourses. The gospel writer arranges the teaching and message of Jesus to place Christ as the one to whom Moses points. Matthew brings us the Sermon on the Mount,[37] the commissioning of the twelve apostles,[38] the parables of the kingdom,[39] teaching on greatness and community life,[40] and teaching on the end times.[41]

8 Great Moses and the greater Jesus in the Sermon on the Mount

Moses held the highest prominence and significance in Israel's story – as a teacher, a prophet and a king. After his death, the closing words of Deuteronomy remind us of this:

> Never since has there arisen a prophet in Israel like Moses, whom the LORD knew face to face. He was unequalled for all the signs and wonders that the LORD sent him to perform in

the land of Egypt, against Pharaoh and all his servants and his entire land, and for all the mighty deeds and all the terrifying displays of power that Moses performed in the sight of all Israel.
(Deuteronomy 34.10–12)

Knowing this, Matthew's gospel not only presents Jesus as a lens through which Moses can be seen and the one to whom Moses points, but also positions Jesus as superior to Moses, particularly in the Sermon on the Mount. We will look at the content of the Sermon on the Mount in the next part of *Flipped*, but it is vitally important to see how Matthew locates Jesus in the kingdom before we turn our attention to the teaching of Jesus that Matthew confronts us with.

King Jesus, Moses and Torah

As Matthew brings us to the first major discourse in his gospel, he has already established the messianic, Davidic, kingly and covenantal credentials of Jesus, but his remarkable account of the teaching of Jesus leaves us in no doubt who is speaking to us. As Matthew records Jesus sitting on the mountainside, the gospel writer tells us that 'he began to speak, and taught them, saying . . .'[42] At the end of the Sermon on the Mount, Matthew records the significance of Jesus' teaching:

Now when Jesus had finished saying these things, the crowds were astounded at his teaching, for he taught them as one having authority, and not as their scribes.
(Matthew 7.28–29)

This teacher–king is unlike any other that Israel has ever known, including Moses. Two elements of what Matthew says make that abundantly clear.

1 Jesus' relationship to Torah

Matthew records Jesus as telling us his relationship to Torah, Israel's 'Law':

> Do not think that I have come to abolish the law or the prophets; I have come not to abolish but to fulfil. For truly I tell you, until heaven and earth pass away, not one letter, not one stroke of a letter, will pass from the law until all is accomplished. Therefore, whoever breaks one of the least of these commandments, and teaches others to do the same, will be called least in the kingdom of heaven; but whoever does them and teaches them will be called great in the kingdom of heaven. For I tell you, unless your righteousness exceeds that of the scribes and Pharisees, you will never enter the kingdom of heaven.
> (Matthew 5.17–20)

Torah, in the hearts and minds of the Jewish people, was not simply a set of rules and regulations to be observed; rather, 'The Law defined the identity of the Jewish People.'[43] Judaism could be seen as resting on three pillars: God, Torah and Israel's identity as God's chosen people.[44] Torah was as central to Jewish identity as our consciousness is to our self-understanding. It provided a worldview within which Jews could understand God, themselves, the world and their place in it.[45]

> The Law was clearly central in all streams of Jewish faith, and the reading of the Law had primacy in the synagogue; it was the role of the Law to regulate Jewish life and practice.[46]

It is probable that at the time of Matthew's writing, the Jewish community was accusing Christians of usurping Torah or trivializing it and seeing it as null and void for their life and their faith.

It is to this idea that Matthew directly speaks, as he records Jesus addressing this very issue. Christ has not come to renounce or repudiate Torah, nor has he come to abolish it. Rather, he has come to fulfil it. In fact, every last detail of Torah, every jot and tittle (the English language equivalent is every dot of an 'i' and cross of a 't') still matters. Jesus is clear – the whole of Torah remains 'until all is accomplished',[47] and no one whom Jesus teaches or who claims to be a follower of Jesus can ignore Torah.[48] In fact, Matthew's account here not only nullifies the accusation that followers of Jesus disregarded Torah, but also highlights the exceptionally high bar that Jesus himself sets. Unless every part of Torah is observed and held in the very highest of regard, then those who claim to honour it are themselves guilty of disregarding it. His words are biting:

> For I tell you, unless your righteousness exceeds that of the scribes and Pharisees, you will never enter the kingdom of heaven.
> (Matthew 5.20)

How, then, does the Torah remain in its place in the ministry of Jesus and in the lives of his followers? This is where we see the remarkable claim that Jesus is making. He has come to fulfil Torah.[49] This does not simply mean that he has come to add to it, to replace it with a new law of love or even with a law that transcends it. Jesus is saying much more than that.[50] Jesus is making a claim to be the living embodiment of Torah, the incarnate and lived-out reality of all that it means to obey Torah and to live in right relationship with God. As King of the kingdom, he is not simply an adherent of Torah; he is Torah, and to live in him, to follow him, to be his disciple, is to live out the principles of Torah in a more profound and meaningful way than any previous understanding of it may offer.

2 A revelation of Torah

The teaching that follows these words is not a re-interpretation of Torah; it is a revelation of what Torah has *always been*. Jesus, in himself, ties the strands of Judaism and salvation together. He *is* Israel – obedient and faithful. He *is* fully human, the new Adam. He *is* God, bringing human and divine into one place. He *is* King. He *is* Messiah. He *is* David's greater Son. He *is* the one to whom Moses points. That is why the righteousness that he demands outstrips that of the Pharisees and the Sadducees, and why the least in his kingdom is the greatest. In effect, Jesus sits with his disciples and makes the most audacious of claims. He tells them that they may have previously read Torah, discussed it, applied it, tried to obey it, sought to plumb its depths and hold on to its principles, but in his very being he *is* Torah, with all its possibilities and beauty.

There follows a series of six summary explorations of the law of Moses[51] in which Jesus returns to one simple phrase that has just as much explosive power as what we have just discovered about Torah. In each of the six examples that Jesus gives, he uses the same phrase:

> You have heard that it was said . . . But I say to you . . .
> (Matthew 5.21–22, 27–28, 31–32, 33–34, 38–39, 43–44)

Rabbis would establish their authority and their authenticity by quoting Moses. Having established that they were grounded in the teaching of the great rabbi himself, they would then quote rabbis who had followed down through the centuries of Judaism, with the phrase, 'And . . . said,' quoting the subsequent rabbis. Depending on the school of rabbinic thought, they would walk through the teaching of the previous generations until they reached their own interpretation, at which point they would simply say, 'And I say to you . . .'

Note that they would not say, 'But I say to you,' because to do so would be to disconnect themselves from the very line of authentication that they were seeking to claim. If they were not connected to previous rabbis, they could not be connected to Moses, the great rabbi. Jesus audaciously quotes Moses, then misses the rabbis who followed Moses, and instead of adding his thoughts at the end of the rabbinic thread, with, 'And I say to you,' he offers the bold, expansive and revolutionary, 'But I say to you.' In so doing he is making a claim about his own ministry and his own interpretation of Torah. He is either throwing Moses and the rabbis who followed Moses out with the bathwater or he is making a bold claim to bring a deeper, fuller and more faithful understanding of Torah to those whom he leads.

Since we know from Matthew 5.17–20 that he is not throwing Torah out, but fulfilling it, we read the rest of Matthew 5 with the dawning realization that Jesus is bringing the fullest revelation and understanding of God that is possible. He is not only telling his listeners what Torah means, but also opening their eyes to see what it has always meant, and he is laying claim to their allegiance to his life, mission and teaching as the new Moses, the great rabbi, the Messiah.

To cement this remarkable presentation, Matthew tells us that Jesus finishes each section of his teaching with some of the most challenging words in the New Testament:

Be perfect, therefore, as your heavenly Father is perfect.
(Matthew 5.48)

But strive first for the kingdom of God and his righteousness, and all these things will be given to you as well.
(Matthew 6.33)

In everything do to others as you would have them do to you; for this is the law and the prophets.
(Matthew 7.12)

Jesus is the living embodiment of the rule and the reign of God. He invites followers from the most ostracized and excluded parts of society. His rule is for the sick, not the healthy. His kingdom is for the uninvited, the overlooked and those who have been told by everyone else that they are not good enough, they are not holy enough, they are not faithful enough. He invites those whose faces don't fit and whose pasts are too chequered, to come and eat with him and to be citizens in his kingdom. He dismisses the legalism, control and smallness of the Pharisees' and Sadducees' understanding of the kingdom of God throughout the gospel of Matthew, painting with bigger strokes and more vibrant colours the hope and freedom that is found in a life with God. In his excoriating attack on their manipulation in Matthew 23, Jesus makes it clear that the righteousness of the leaders of Israel is nothing but dead people's bones compared with the life that being one of his followers brings. That is why he tells his listeners to stay in direct connection with him – the King of the kingdom.

> But you are not to be called rabbi, for you have one teacher, and you are all students. And call no one your father on earth, for you have one Father – the one in heaven. Nor are you to be called instructors, for you have one instructor, the Messiah. The greatest among you will be your servant. All who exalt themselves will be humbled, and all who humble themselves will be exalted.
> (Matthew 23.8–12)

His words here are not about who we call our biological dads, nor are they about unhealthy rebelliousness and arrogance that refuses to be accountable or eschews teachability. Rather, they are a reminder that every single follower of Jesus is called into a direct and living relationship with the King, whose kingdom and reign will never end because 'he will reign over the house of Jacob for ever, and of his kingdom there will be no end'.[52]

We have covered a lot of ground as we have explored Matthew's scope and understanding of Jesus as King, particularly the ways in which he positions Jesus as the one to whom Moses points. By positioning Jesus in this way, Matthew is telling his audience that Jesus is their Prophet, their Priest, their King, their Rabbi, their Teacher, their Hope, their Messiah, their Saviour, their Deliverer, their Lord and their King. He alone can demand their loyalty and their devotion.

As we mentioned earlier, in the middle of his gospel, Matthew records John the Baptist, Jesus' cousin, asking a question about who Jesus is. Imprisoned, alone and frightened, the once convinced John sends messengers to Jesus, asking, 'Are you the one who is to come, or are we to wait for another?'[53]

Jesus replies by pointing to what is happening through his ministry, telling the messengers they are to tell John what they 'hear and see':

> The blind receive their sight, the lame walk, the lepers are
> cleansed, the deaf hear, the dead are raised, and the poor have
> good news brought to them. And blessed is anyone who takes
> no offence at me.
> (Matthew 11.4–6)

I wonder if we often ask the same question – is Jesus 'the one', or are we waiting for 'another'?

What Jesus as King means for us today

Where we see it working

How do we capture all these truths and challenges in a way that makes sense today? To try to do that, reflect with me for a moment on the impact of the Covid pandemic on the church in the United

Kingdom. I am being specific in locating our discussion there because I want to avoid unhelpful generalizations and misrepresentations. I do not want to look at a range of statistics and ideas about how the church has fared across this period in the United Kingdom either. I want to reflect on a few of the things that I have seen during this time, as a pastor, a theologian and an individual follower of Jesus.

There have been plenty of negative stories about Christians giving up on church during the last few years. Wearied by the disappointment of these years, some have decided that the faith they thought they had was not as meaningful as they had once assumed, and they have discovered that they can do quite well without church. I make no comment on that. I have, however, seen something else.

Some, who have found this season equally as difficult, have reimagined the claims of Jesus on their lives. They have tried to think again about the rule and the reign of God in their lives. It is true that some of them have stopped 'going' to church, but many of them have also started 'being' the church. I have a few friends who have stepped away from the structures and programmes of church as we once knew them, but who have stepped into life-giving community, mission and purpose.

I am not talking here about those who have deconstructed everything and now spend their time cynically dismissing other Christians and local churches. It is one thing to reflect on a structure because it is broken, but it is quite another to inhabit a place of permanent sneering. There are great examples of people who have found the Covid pandemic difficult but who have pressed into the lordship of Jesus during this time.

Jenny's new journey

Jenny[54] entered Covid battling mental-health issues, burdened and weary after a battle with cancer. Her engagement with church during lockdown was sporadic and eventually she stopped participating altogether. I chatted with her about her struggles and challenges and encouraged her to reconsider her decision to drop out of Christian community. I suggested that we might read the book of Ephesians together and chat about what it looked like to live for the Jesus we discover in it – the one who is head of his church, gives gifts to his people and calls us to lives of faithfulness. She thought this was a good idea and agreed to meet with me (sometimes in a physical place, sometimes online) as a means of staying in touch.

Over a period of around 18 months, I saw her capture a vision of the reign and the rule of Jesus in her life in a new way. She stopped worrying about attending church and started focusing on what it means for her to be church and be in Christian fellowship. She left the church community she was part of, recognizing that it had not been the right place for her for some time.

Around the same time, she started a small charity to help people who were struggling with isolation, rooted in the teaching and example and the demands of Jesus. That small charity is helping a couple of dozen people every week. Jenny is now part of a small house fellowship that does not meet in conventional ways but is very intentional about living out the call of Jesus. She loves it. Jenny has left the building, but she has not left the church. She is more focused, more fruitful and more faithful than she has been for years. All because of an invitation to consider. Jenny is living under the kingship of Jesus in new and exciting ways.

A pastor's new passion

In February 2014, Russia invaded the Donbas and was largely ignored by the West, but in February 2022 Vladimir Putin sent his forces into a full assault on Ukraine. The world reacted in horror. Sanctions, interventions and embargoes have followed. Amid all that uncertainty, though, many Christians have been getting involved. They understand that the kingship of Jesus means that their sisters and brothers in Ukraine need help, and they have been willing to put their own comforts aside to demonstrate solidarity to others.

Not far from where I am writing, one local church pastor was so moved by what he saw that he spoke to his church leadership team about it. He was convinced that a shared Saviour meant that he should be reaching out to churches and church leaders in Ukraine to offer them help and support. He didn't know any Ukrainians, he didn't speak Ukrainian and he had no idea what he could do to help, but he knew that if Jesus were in his shoes, he would be using his resources and his time to do something to assist. So that is what this local pastor did.

We are now almost eight months down the road. His church sports hall is now a set of bedrooms and apartments for Ukrainians, his home is now shared with six Ukrainians and his church congregation is hosting, welcoming and supporting 42 people from Ukraine. Through them, the church community is also supporting hundreds more men and women in Ukraine and the surrounding countries, helping them to find ways of not only surviving but also making a life.

The motivation for all of this came from the words of Jesus:

'Lord, when was it that we saw you hungry and gave you food, or thirsty and gave you something to drink? And when was it that we saw you a stranger and welcomed you, or naked and gave you clothing? And when was it that we saw you sick or in prison and visited you?' And the king will answer them, 'Truly I tell you, just as you did it to one of the least of these who are members of my family, you did it to me.'
(Matthew 25.37–40)

The challenges and possibilities of Jesus as King

Challenges

The claims and challenges that Matthew places before his original readers are placed before us too. Somehow, in the centuries following Moses, the Jewish people relied more and more on their codification of the law than they did on the giver of the law. For all the right reasons – desires to be holy, faithful and distinct among them – they added more and more expectations. The idea of a king became more important than the king himself.

They made the mistakes that we often make too. Rather than facing the present reality of their lives, their culture and their context, they either looked back wistfully or forward in desperation. Their faith became deeply embedded in what they once were or what they were going to be and they missed the rich, beautiful possibility of how they were called to live in the here and now. They were God's people in name, in culture and even in self-identification, but they had lost sight of the power that this reality brought to them. Are we any different?

Mickey Cohen was a famous gangster in the United States of America in the 1950s. He was invited to a church service by some Christians because they believed that if he were to become a Christian, he would have an enormous impact on many people. Eventually he agreed to yield his life to Christ, but changed little about his life.

> Hopes ran high among his believing acquaintances. But with the passing of time no one could detect any change in Cohen's life. Finally they confronted him with the reality that being a Christian meant he would have to give up his friends and his profession. Cohen demurred. His logic? There are Christian football players, Christian cowboys, Christian politicians; why not a Christian gangster?[55]

Cohen's response is emblematic of the challenge that the kingship of Jesus presents to those who claim to follow him. His reign and rule must look like something in our lives. The reality is that Christ's reign and rule not only announces something to the world – that God has broken in, that sin and shame and guilt are dealt with and that pain does not have the last word – but it also invites us. It invites the broken, the forgotten and the excluded, and it also invites those who think they have it all together to recognize that they do not, and those who think they are powerful to lay down their self-appointed status as guardians of the gospel or custodians of the truth.

Jesus makes demands of his followers that we cannot ignore. He is not simply a sage or a rabbi; he is the divine King, who presents 'strenuous commands' to his people.[56] We do not have a king who was temporarily reigning but one who is permanently enthroned. He is not a localized rural figure of the first century. His words echo and reverberate into every culture and context and demand a response. His lack of political power or influence does not imply that we should not be politically or socially engaged, because he calls us, as our King, to be salt and light in the world. His message is not simply 'spiritual' in a sense that negates actual-change-in-the-here-and-now. He does not enter our world only so that we can go to heaven when we die. He enters our world to change it and to call a kingdom of people to his side who will do his will, announce his reign, live out his priorities and change the world.[57]

The kingship of Jesus must look like something in our lives, or it means nothing at all. His claim to be King demands a response from us – spiritually, physically, financially, religiously, socially, politically, morally, ethically, economically, environmentally, relationally, sexually, interpersonally and in every other way we can imagine. There is not a single area of our lives that is not affected by his claim to reign.[58]

Jesus' kingship is not a multiple-choice menu from which we get to decide the bits we want and the bits we do not want. To recognize his kingship affects everything in our lives. There is, perhaps, one passage above all others in the gospel of Matthew that reminds us of the extent of this call. Matthew strategically places it just before the Transfiguration. I wonder if his reason for doing so is to give us a reality check? We may want the glory and the excitement of a transfiguration experience, but are we willing to carry the cross? The truth is, we cannot have one without the other.

> Then Jesus told his disciples, 'If any want to become my followers, let them deny themselves and take up their cross and follow me. For those who want to save their life will lose it, and those who lose their life for my sake will find it. For what will it profit them if they gain the whole world but forfeit their life? Or what will they give in return for their life?' (Matthew 16.24–26)

Cross bearing was not popular during Jesus' earthly ministry, and it is still not popular today. It remains the fact, however, that King Jesus was hoisted on to a cruel piece of torture apparatus. The throne that was raised above Jerusalem was not made of gold; it was made of wood. The crown placed on his brow was not one of diamonds and jewels or even laurel leaves; it was made of thorns. His earthly coronation was not filled with adulation and appreciation; it was filled with sneering crowds and cries to crucify him. There was no celebration and rejoicing when he took his place; there was sorrow and heartbreak in the lives of his followers. His visible life on earth began in poverty and obscurity and ended in humiliation and death, yet he was still King. Nothing changed that. Even the attempt to mock him at the end with a cheap wooden sign nailed above his head announced the truth of who he was:

This is Jesus, the King of the Jews.
(Matthew 27.37)

King of the Jews? King of the world? Our King? What does that mean for us right here and right now?

Possibilities

What if the kingship of Jesus is an invitation to us to reimagine and reshape our lives in ways that bring new colour and vibrancy to his life in us?

My conversion and my call to pastoral and preaching ministry happened in the very same moment. On a cold February evening in 1986, as I left the Whitewell Church building, located half-way up the Whitewell Road in Belfast, with the words of Pastor James McConnell ringing in my ears, I knew that if I surrendered to Christ, it would change the direction of my life entirely. As a 16-year-old boy, I was faced with the demands of God's Son. If I followed him, it would mean surrender, obedience and sacrifice. It would not be easy, and a life of comfort and applause was not part of the deal. I knew that. As I surrendered my life to God that night, I was laying down any rights and offering God my whole life. This is what conversion is.

I have tried to take back control of my life so many times – and God has let me. I have failed God. I have said no to God. I have fought with God. I have learned, the hard way, that a temporarily surrendered life does not lead to a fulfilled life. Each time I have wrestled with God and demanded my own way, God has waited for me. I am grateful for divine grace and mercy. The call, however, has never changed. If I am to follow Christ, then it involves the surrender of everything to God. What that looks like changes depending on our stage of life and what is around us, but surrender is still the key.

My wife Debbie and I have known God's rich grace through the last few years. In many ways they have been tough. Debbie's dad continues to decline in health because of long-term dementia. My brother is currently in end-of-life care and about to come to live with us for the last few months that he has. We've both been badly hit with Covid, with Debbie suffering from long Covid and me being fitted with a pacemaker because of it. It hasn't been easy. The pressures of church life, disappointment relating to those who have walked away, the heartbreak of a staff member leaving our team right at the beginning of this season have all taken their toll.

But we have also been blessed during this time. We have seen shedloads of people starting to attend and be part of our church family, our leadership team has been incredible, I have had the privilege of joining the Irish leadership team of my denomination, and a few national and global initiatives that I have been involved in have really grown. Since Covid began we have moved house, our son has married his fiancée and moved house, our daughter has graduated from university and we have become grandparents four times! It certainly hasn't all been bad.

During all of this, Debbie and I have felt a nudge to try to set up a retreat centre for weary leaders and couples. We've seen what happens when leaders, pastors, missionaries, charity CEOs and many others get burned out or hurt. We've watched some of our closest friends being treated badly by church leadership teams. We've wept as so many have been snubbed, sacked or pushed out. As we made that journey with so many, we were reminded that our own callings are not just professional career placements. We have been thrilled to deepen our love of Jesus and our love of one another over these last years and we have found ourselves thinking about what we can do with our whole lives in a much more intentional way.

As we prayed about the experiences we have had, the resources we have been entrusted with and the passions in our hearts, as a couple we felt that God wanted us to create a space for others to come and be strengthened and ministered to. It will be our home, but it will also be a home for others who need it, without cost and without long-term expectations. We're looking at ways it can be used for grief counselling, couple support, ministry in prayer, worship evenings, releasing new gifts and encouraging new ventures – all for Jesus. It won't be a denominational thing. It won't be owned by one church or one community. It will simply be us living open and welcoming lives in a space that has enough room for others to be blessed. Why? Because we are trying to take seriously the call of Jesus to serve his people and to love the broken. It hasn't happened yet, but we are ready for it. In spite of three house sale collapses since we began, we are hopeful that the lordship of Christ will flow through us to others and that God's kingdom will be extended through what we are trying to do.

There are probably thousands of you who have similar stories. Unnoticed women and men who are just trying to live your lives for your King. Good on you! Don't give up. Don't get bogged down in all the things that you know won't work. Ask yourself what life might look like for you as a citizen of the upside-down kingdom. Debbie and I are hoping to carry on what we are planning now right through into our retirement and beyond. We don't want our names in lights – we just want to be a blessing, because in the kingdom that Jesus came to advance, the lost find a home and the lonely find a family. If we can do something to make those ideas and beliefs realities, it is worth a shot, don't you think?

What if the kingship of Jesus is an invitation to us to reimagine and reshape our lives in ways that bring new colour and vibrancy to his life in us?

Let's pray

Lord and King,
We pause in this moment and open our hands before you. We thank you for your reign and rule in our lives and in the world. We are grateful for your patience with us and for your promises to us. We

know that you are our friend, our confidant, our hope, our strength and our song. We know that you have lifted us when we have fallen, forgiven us when we have failed and restored us when we have tarnished your name – thank you. In this moment, however, and in the daily choices of our lives, we ask that you would help us to serve you as our King.

Help us to bow before you.

Help us to listen to you.

Help us to be obedient to you.

Help us to live consistently for your kingdom.

Forgive us when we put our priorities at the top of your agenda instead of letting your priorities shape our agendas.

Forgive us when we make your kingship look like our politics and outlook.

Forgive us when we baptize our theologies and justify our prejudices in your name.

Help us to rediscover the power of a surrendered life.

Do what you want with us.

Send us where you want.

Set us to what you want.

Use us as you see fit.

Write straight with the crooked lines of our lives, Lord.

As voices around us declare that they are our king, help us to live for you, the True King.

As our own wills tell us that we are in charge, help us to surrender to you, the True King.

In a world that says, 'Be your own king,' help us to live with you as our King.

King Jesus, help our lives to reflect your life.

King Jesus, help our actions to point to you.

King Jesus, help us live as citizens of your kingdom on earth,

Now and every day.

Amen.

2

People of the kingdom

The world says, 'Chase popularity.'
Jesus says, 'Welcome everybody.'

Blessed are the poor in spirit, for theirs is the kingdom of
heaven . . .
   Blessed are those who are persecuted for righteousness'
sake, for theirs is the kingdom of heaven.
(Matthew 5.3, 10)

Children look at things very directly and simply. I did not
see anyone taking off his coat and giving it to the poor. I
didn't see anyone having a banquet and calling in the lame,
the halt (*sic*), and the blind. And those who were doing it,
like the Salvation Army, did not appeal to me. I wanted,
though I did not know it then, a synthesis. I wanted life and
I wanted abundant life. I wanted it for others too. I did not
want just the few, the missionary-minded people like the
Salvation Army, to be kind to the poor as the poor. I wanted
everyone to be kind. I wanted every home to be open to the
lame, the halt (*sic*), and the blind . . . Only then did people
really live, really love their brothers (*sic*). In such love as the
abundant life, and I did not have the slightest idea how to
find it.
(Dorothy Day)[1]

Paulo,[2] with a smile that filled the world, eyes as big as saucers and
a laugh like a virus of hope, invited me into a life that I had never

71

imagined and could never have planned. He changed me, and I am glad that he did.

Just after I became a Christian, I was invited to visit Mexico and spend time there on a ranch called Sparrows Gate that was being run for children who were either orphaned or extremely poor.[3] The visit transformed me. We slept in a converted pigsty, with a staple diet of refried beans and water. Dean Tinney had begun the work not long before I went there. Previously a wealthy American businessman, Dean had been challenged by the teaching of Jesus in the Sermon on the Mount to do something about the lives of the children who were struggling to survive in the Tijuana area of Mexico, just across the border from where Dean had lived in a prosperous and leafy part of San Diego. He ploughed all he had into the mission.

Sparrows Gate

There was very little spare money and not a lot of resources at Sparrows Gate, but there was indescribable beauty and uncontainable hope. This was where I met Paulo. He was only a few years old when he had been left in an abandoned car by his parents, as far as we knew. He had come to Sparrows Gate as a frightened, hungry and confused little boy, and slowly he was being changed by the love and kindness of the place. Dean and his team sought to show every child in their care the kindness and compassion that they believed Jesus called his people to display.

The ranch's name is based on the words of the third verse of Psalm 84, because the team want to show every child in their care the love of Jesus and teach them about him. It's a beautiful display of what kingdom life can look like. This upside-down community honours the abandoned and welcomes the weak, making room in their hearts and at their table for those the world has either turned their back on or never noticed in the first place.

The minute Paulo and I saw each other, there was a connection. His eyes tried to tell the story of the tough life that he was learning to survive, and they betrayed a determination and passion that was remarkable. I don't know why he and I connected more fully than I did with the other children. Maybe a shared sadness? Maybe a soul connection because we somehow both understood the pain and the difficulty that childhood can bring? Of course, I can only figure that out looking back. During the few weeks that we spent together, we were both too young to work out such things. I was just a teenager and he was just a small boy. We communicated by writing in the sand, by pointing, by smiles and nods and lots of other non-verbal engagement.

When it came time to leave Mexico and return to Northern Ireland, I was devastated to leave him, and he was heartbroken to see me go. He called me 'Papa'. I still hear his voice in my head sometimes. I smile as I remember him, and I pray for him. I cry. I miss him. He became a physical expression of what I understood God was calling me into.

My time with Paulo and the other children at Sparrows Gate taught me so much about what it means to be a citizen of the kingdom of heaven. He just wanted to be seen, to be known and to be heard. He did not want my money (I had none), but he did need physical support – the food, the warmth, the security and the education that Sparrows Gate was providing. His dignity was not in his possessions or his standing or his education; it was in his humanity. The most precious things that we shared were friendship, honesty and hope. Our time together was a gift to both of us. Our shared humanity, our shared experiences of life and our shared desire to grasp hold of life created bonds that were quickly established and can still conjure up emotion and love in me today, almost forty years after I met him.

My grandchildren call me 'Papa'. It is only as I write now that I wonder if my choice of that word was rooted in the sense of tenderness and relationship that I had with Paulo. I think maybe it was.

The community at Sparrows Gate was a living expression of the lives that are described in the opening words of the Sermon on the Mount.

Blessed are the poor in spirit, for theirs is the kingdom of heaven.

Blessed are those who mourn, for they will be comforted.

Blessed are the meek, for they will inherit the earth.

Blessed are those who hunger and thirst for righteousness, for they will be filled.

Blessed are the merciful, for they will receive mercy.

Blessed are the pure in heart, for they will see God.

Blessed are the peacemakers, for they will be called children of God.

Blessed are those who are persecuted for righteousness' sake, for theirs is the kingdom of heaven.

Blessed are you when people revile you and persecute you and utter all kinds of evil against you falsely on my account. Rejoice and be glad, for your reward is great in heaven, for in the same way they persecuted the prophets who were before you. (Matthew 5.3–12)

At the ranch, not only did the children find a home and a safe place, but they also found a community that saw their dignity, worth and beauty and sought to acknowledge it in acts of mercy and kindness. The volunteers were also transformed. This community wept with the weeping, gave space and time and agency to the marginalized and fed both the spiritual and physical needs of those who were part of it. They were opposed by many in the wider community, criticized as do-gooders and mocked for wasting their time, but that didn't stop them.

In that community, I experienced the reality of what Christian family is supposed to be. Away from platforms and big names, I encountered the transforming power of what it means to *be* God's people. There is much to learn from them. Surrounded, as we so often are, with a culture that says we should chase popularity, be seen with the right people, like the influencers and walk with the powerful, Jesus calls us to open our hearts and our lives to everybody who has need and to show the world that we are his people by loving the people he puts before us. That can be hard, but it can also be liberating.

Dorothy Day

Dorothy Day (1897–1980) came to faith as a 30-year-old woman. She was searching for purpose all her life. She wanted more than the culture around her offered. She wanted to live in a way that was genuinely life-giving, both to herself and to those around her. She read great novelists, engaged in cultural pursuits, joined the socialist movement. She became increasingly concerned that 'in her community, the destitute had always been looked upon as shiftless, worthless, without talent of any kind, all because of their own fault'.[4] On one occasion, when she was imprisoned in Washington for protests she was involved with, she wrote of the upside-down way in which she saw the world because of her faith:

All through those first weary days in jail when I was in solitary confinement, the only thoughts that brought comfort to my were soul were those lines in the Psalms that expressed the terror and misery of man (*sic*) suddenly stricken and abandoned. Solitude and hunger and weariness of spirit – those sharpened my perceptions so that I suffered not only my own sorrow but the sorrows of those about me. I was no longer a young girl, part of a radical movement seeking justice for those oppressed; I was the oppressed. I was that drug addict screaming and tossing in her cell, beating her head against the wall.[5]

Day turned away from her faith, however, after her time in prison, because she did not know how she could make sense of the pain and the sorrow of the world in a church that she felt was ineffective and disconnected. She later wrote of her sense of desolation at the pain of the world. She felt like she would never be free because she would always know that there were men and women trapped in poverty and carrying the weight of social and economic injustice.[6] She discovered her purpose in the Catholic Church and particularly in the Benedictine tradition with its emphasis on being present with and to the poor and living in simple devotion and dependence upon God. It was Catholic social teaching that was to become the bedrock of her understanding of her purpose and eventually led to her beginning a new newspaper called *Catholic Worker.*[7]

What Dorothy Day's ministry and the work of Sparrows Gate share is their commitment to a radical and rooted lifestyle that flows from the teaching and example of Jesus. They take seriously the social, ethical and practical teaching of Christ and they see in his instructions a call to a completely different way of looking at the world, both individually as one of his followers and collectively as part of his church and his kingdom. In Matthew's gospel, Jesus' five discourses[8] set out many of the attributes of this countercultural lifestyle and worldview. In this section of *Flipped*, I want to focus on Jesus' teaching in the Sermon on the Mount and explore what it means to people of the kingdom.

The Sermon on the Mount

I have been captivated by the Sermon on the Mount from the first time I read it in 1986. It is contained in chapters 5 to 7 of Matthew's gospel. Since then, I have returned to it at least once a month, every month. I have no doubt that it is the most influential piece of writing in my life and that I will spend the rest of my life trying to understand it, submit to it and live it out. I have preached on it many times, referred to it thousands more and referenced it in every book I have ever written. This is the first time I have attempted to capture the sense of the whole sermon in one place, but it will not be the last.[9] In the words of D. A. Carson:

> The more I read these three chapters . . . the more I am both drawn to them and shamed by them. Their brilliant light draws me like a moth to a spotlight; but the light is so bright that it sears and burns. No room is left for forms of piety which are nothing more than veneer and sham. Perfection is demanded.[10]

In many ways, Matthew's record of the Sermon on the Mount is the litmus test of Christian faith. Scott McKnight describes it as 'the moral portrait of Jesus' own people'.[11] How we respond to it is a strong indicator of the depths, and the genuineness, of our conversion.

These words stir the soul, they reach into the very centre of our lives and do three primary things. First, they confront us with the best way to live, shown in Christ and in his teaching here. Second, they hold a mirror up to our souls and let us see how much room there is for growth in our own lives and in the church. Third, they spark (or should) a yearning for a greater ability to live as God has called us. Commenting on the fourth beatitude, which promises that those who hunger and thirst after righteousness will be filled,[12] Martyn Lloyd-Jones speaks of how we might assess its impact on us:

> I do not know of a better test that anyone can apply to himself or herself in this whole matter of the Christian profession

than a verse like this. If this verse is to you one of the most blessed statements of the whole of Scripture, you can be quite certain you are a Christian; if it is not then you had better examine the foundations again.[13]

Jesus' words here are not to be sugar-coated and sanitized into aspirations for the future that make us feel warm and hopeful on the inside but which we can ignore in the here and now. We cannot afford to trivialize them in this way, because doing so would denude us of a powerful motivation for transformation in our daily lives through continual dependence on the Holy Spirit.

We cannot allow the words of Jesus here to crush us either. This has happened too often. Pinchas Lapide, an orthodox Jew, wrote a brief commentary on the Sermon on the Mount in which he commented on this dangerous tendency:

> In fact, the history of the impact of the Sermon on the Mount can largely be described in terms of an attempt to domesticate everything in it that is shocking, demanding, and uncompromising, and render it harmless.[14]

I am convinced that the message that Matthew records for us here is not one of inevitable condemnation and failure because the expectations are too high, but rather they invite us into a threefold awareness. They show us what being human can really look like; they invite us to be honest about our absolute inability to live in this way in our own strength; and they beckon us into a higher place of openness to and dependence upon the Spirit of God at work in our lives *in the here and now*. This was the basis of how Dietrich Bonhoeffer came to understand the Sermon on the Mount, which largely shaped his classic work, *The Cost of Discipleship*. In his preface to the 2001 edition of the book, John W. De Gruchy outlines how Bonhoeffer came to see the Sermon on the Mount:

Instead of regarding Jesus' sermon in the way that had become traditional for Lutherans, that is, as a 'law' that condemns us and so prepares us to receive the 'gospel' of grace, Bonhoeffer came to see that the Sermon on the Mount was a charter for life lived by grace.[15]

If we want to be kingdom people, then the Sermon on the Mount must make its way into our hearts, into our souls and into our imaginations. It must shape our thinking, our being and our doing. In short, these words of Jesus must captivate us. And when they do, we will never be able to live well without returning to them again and again for comfort, for challenge and for hope.

Before you do anything else, please take around 20 minutes and read Matthew chapters 5, 6 and 7. Find a quiet place where you can concentrate, bring a cup of something with you and open your Bible. Read this Sermon. Take a notepad and pen and, if you can, write down what immediately springs to mind as you're reading. If you have another 20 minutes, read it again. Allow it to start to percolate into your soul. Let it find a resting place in your heart. But beware. The seed of these words, once planted in your life, will mean that you will never be the same again. Ask God to help you not only to read these words, but also to start to understand them; and ask God to let these words read you.

The Sermon on the Mount is probably the best-known part of the teaching of Jesus, though arguably it is the least understood, and certainly it is the least obeyed. It is the nearest thing to a manifesto that he ever uttered, for it is his own description of what he wanted his followers to be and to do. To my mind, no two words sum up its intention better, or indicate more clearly its challenge to the modern world, than the expression 'Christian counter-culture.'[16]

From Augustine of Hippo (AD 354–430), who described it as 'a perfect standard of the Christian life', to Dallas Willard's (1935–2013) provocative unpacking of its teaching in *The Divine Conspiracy*,[17] Matthew's account of Jesus' words has captivated and challenged the imaginations of Christians of every generation. In it we read of the flipped kingdom that is the subject of this book. Matthew paints a picture of what should characterize the people of the kingdom through Jesus' teaching contained here. We cannot be people of the kingdom without coming face to face with this Sermon, as it is recorded in this gospel.

> Jesus' good news, then, was that the Kingdom of God had come, and that he, Jesus, was its herald and expounder to men. More than that, in some special, mysterious way, he was the Kingdom.[18]

In this volume, I am not going to explore the myriad ways in which the Sermon on the Mount has been dissected, discussed and defined by commentators over the years. There are plenty of places where you can explore such topics.[19] It is sufficient for our purposes that I state how I will approach the text of Matthew 5—7.

I will treat this as Matthew's particular summary of teaching, delivered by Jesus on a Galilean hillside to his listening disciples. I do not intend to explore its relationship to the Sermon on the Plain in Luke 6 other than to say that I am aware of the vast discussion of the relationship between the two texts.[20] My purpose here is to set out a way of engaging with the Sermon on the Mount by exploring just the first part of it – Matthew 5 – and then considering, with you, what the implications of it are for us as kingdom people.

The Sermon on the Mount in context and the authority of Jesus

Matthew frames the Sermon for us by giving us almost identical summary statements on either side of it. Remember that the original text did not have verses or chapters, so this literary technique would have helped those hearing his words to understand that everything contained within those summary statements was to be understood as a cohesive unit.

> Jesus went through Galilee, teaching in their synagogues and proclaiming the good news of the kingdom and curing every disease and every sickness among the people. So his fame spread throughout all Syria, and they brought to him all the sick, those who were afflicted with various diseases and pains, demoniacs, epileptics, and paralytics, and he cured them. And great crowds followed him from Galilee, the Decapolis, Jerusalem, Judea, and from beyond the Jordan.
> (Matthew 4.23–25)

> Then Jesus went about all the cities and villages, teaching in their synagogues, and proclaiming the good news of the kingdom, and curing every disease and every sickness.
> (Matthew 9.35)

Everything within these verbal parentheses is to be considered as a single unit, whose purpose is repeated in both scriptures above, namely the proclamation of 'the good news of the kingdom'.

You may wonder why Matthew does not include the summary statement found in 9.35 at the end of chapter 7. Simply put, it is because Matthew frames the Sermon on the Mount *twice*. First, as noted here, he sets the context of this Sermon being centrally linked to the *proclamation* and the *demonstration* of the kingdom of God. Jesus' *proclamation* is contained within Matthew 5—7. The *demonstration* of these kingdom principles is found in both his teaching, the content of the Sermon on the Mount, and in his miraculous activity, which is recorded in Matthew 8 and 9. Second, Matthew frames the Sermon itself with his opening

comments in Matthew 5.1–2 and his closing comments in Matthew
7.28—8.1:

> When Jesus saw the crowds, he went up the mountain; and
> after he sat down, his disciples came to him. Then he began to
> speak, and he taught them, saying . . .
> (Matthew 5.1–2)

> Now when Jesus has finished saying these things, the crowds
> were astounded at his teaching, for he taught them as one
> having authority, and not as their scribes.
> When Jesus had come down from the mountain; great crowds
> followed him.
> (Matthew 7.28—8.1)

When Jesus sees the crowds, he turns his attention to teaching
his disciples. His words have such an impact on those who are his
followers, though, and they are so different from the way the Jewish
people have come to hear the rabbis of their age, that the crowds are
'astounded' at his teaching and the authority with which he speaks.

The second framing that Matthew offers us is of Jesus' teaching
being heard by his followers but spilling over into the wider crowds
that are listening to him. Matthew probes into the impact of Jesus'
teaching by noting the way in which the crowd hears his authoritative instruction. Matthew leaves an invisible question hanging in
the air at the end of the actual proclamation of the Sermon on the
Mount. He invites us to ask how far the authority of Jesus goes. The
answer to this question is found in Matthew 8 and 9, which is why
we have the two sets of framing remarks.

Matthew 8 and 9 is a record of the miraculous ministry of Jesus,
his call upon his followers and the turning of his attention to the harvest that is waiting. As Matthew unfolds it, we have the healing of a
leper;[21] the healing of the centurion's servant;[22] the healing of many

at Peter's house;[23] a challenge to would-be followers;[24] the stilling of a storm;[25] the deliverance of people afflicted with demons;[26] the challenge of his presence being rejected;[27] his demonstration of the power to forgive sins by the healing of a man who could not walk;[28] the calling of Matthew;[29] questions about fasting;[30] the raising of a girl from the dead and the healing of a woman with a menstrual bleed;[31] the healing of two blind men;[32] the healing of a man who was unable to speak;[33] and a call for labourers for the harvest field.[34]

This series of events is a direct and deliberate device used by the gospel writer to show just how deep and how far the authority of Jesus reaches. Having framed the teaching of Jesus with the descriptions of his proclamation and healing, Matthew draws an ever-expanding circle to show his readers the extent of the authority of Christ. Jesus' authority is sufficient to heal a Jewish leper; one step out, and his authority is sufficient to heal a Gentile servant; take another step with Matthew and we see that Jesus can heal many people in a home. At this point, Matthew deliberately pauses his demonstration of the authority of Jesus to remind his audience that there is a cost in following this King. Matthew then picks up his examples again by telling us that Jesus' authority also touches nature and the created world because Jesus can calm a storm. Finally, in chapter 9, we see Jesus' authority over demonic power itself as he sets free two people afflicted with demons. It is an astounding demonstration of the depth and reach of Jesus' authority!

Then we have another significant moment, as Matthew tells us of Jesus being driven out of the town by the people; clearly the authority of this man means that he somehow threatens their security and their ways of life. Then, as if to prove that Jesus is not confined in his power to one small area, we read of him crossing the water and coming to his own town. Matthew then continues his expansive account of the authority of Jesus. Now we are told that

Jesus has the power to forgive sins, and Jesus proves it by healing the man who cannot walk.

The circles continue to widen. He can heal, he can set free, he can calm storms, he can deliver those afflicted by demons and he can forgive sins.

This completes the ever-expanding circle of authority that Matthew is proving – but there is more to come. Jesus has the authority to call people to follow him – he is a rabbi; he has the authority to challenge the religious elite of the day about their customs and their expectation of godliness and faithfulness, which is demonstrated by his response to those who criticize his followers for not fasting. The expansion continues as we see his authority over life and death when he brings a dead girl back to life.

Then we see him reach beyond the respectability barriers that have locked people out of community as he heals a woman considered unclean and outcast because of a menstrual bleed. As she reaches out and touches him, he knows that something has happened because he even has authority to know when someone touches him for healing.

As we approach the end of this section of Matthew's gospel, we witness Jesus being described in messianic terms as the Son of David by the two[35] blind men that he heals. The last miracle recorded is one in which a demon is cast out of a man and the man is given the power of speech again, but the Jewish leaders reject Jesus again, denying any divine power and stating that he is only able to heal by the power of 'the ruler of demons'.[36]

And so Matthew brings us to his outer summary statement again – about the nature of Jesus' proclamation and healing ministry and the demonstration of the kingdom of heaven. Every story Matthew uses is intentional. Jesus' circle of authority is seen in his actions, heard in his teaching and demonstrated in his healing and miraculous interventions. He has the power to heal, to deliver, to set free from evil, to forgive sins, to raise from the dead, to demand allegiance as a rabbi, to restore people into society and community and to challenge the religious elitism of his day. And he has this power because he is the Son of David. Yet the religious leaders still reject him and accuse him of being controlled by evil forces. Even those sneering rejections will not distract Jesus from his mission, however, and we see this section close with Jesus being moved with compassion for the outcast, the helpless and the desperate as he calls his disciples to see the harvest ahead of the opposition.

Before we turn to the content of the Sermon on the Mount itself, just pause and let everything that I have written sink in.

You might need to take a breath.

Jesus' ministry is to the people that his society rejects. He sits with the outcast. He heals the leper. He welcomes the woman who is bleeding. He delivers the demon-afflicted. Can there be any better demonstration of the folk to whom those of us who are kingdom people are called to go? We do not see an elite, separatist and aloof king in Matthew's unfolding story; we see one who is intent on welcoming the outcast. The very people that the Jewish hierarchy rejects are the ones to whom Jesus goes. Not only that, but Matthew's story also lets us see that there is hope for us with Jesus. If Christ goes to these people, he would come to us.

It's remarkable.

An outline of the Sermon on the Mount

In this book, I can do no more than give you a brief outline of what Jesus teaches in the Sermon on the Mount in the hope that it will spark a hunger in you to spend the rest of your life in this remarkable message from the King. What I offer here is my understanding of the Sermon and what it meant for those who heard it, before turning my attention to thinking about what it means for us today, where we see it working, what the challenges are and what possibilities it might present to us.

It is helpful to see the Sermon as one great sweep of teaching with three movements. In Matthew 5, Jesus helps his listeners to understand how God sees them and how they should see themselves. This is the kingdom perspective, and we cover this in chapter 4. In Matthew 6, Jesus challenges them to consider their inner and outer lives in relation to the core devotional practices of Judaism and their individual possessions and how the two are connected. In Matthew 7, he questions the manner in which they make judgements about other people, and he gives them three tests for the authenticity of faith, both their own and that of others. In his Sermon, Jesus flips much of the traditional understanding of his audience, about themselves and about others.

What does it mean for us to be kingdom people today? The challenges and possibilities

The world is undergoing transformation . . . a chaotic period where most anything can happen and little can be predicted; where yesterday's rule takers become tomorrow's rule makers, but no one follows rules anymore; where competing global visions collide with each other; where remnants of the past, present, and future coexist simultaneously.[37]

The world is changing around us and we, the people of God, must work out how to respond to those changes. From the climate catastrophe to national and global conflicts, we are in flux. The Covid pandemic is a 'history accelerating crisis' like many before it.[38] Somehow, we need to find a new way of rooting ourselves during this crisis. We need an identity out of which we can live, a 'new interpretive framework'.[39] The Sermon on the Mount gives exactly this to the people of God. When we see ourselves as kingdom people, we can root our identity in God's purposes and perspectives as our primary soil. The traits and characteristics of God's kingdom then begin to shape our culture and expectations as kingdom people. The implications of this are vast.

Dismantling old structures, finding new ways

Just as the Jews of Jesus' day needed to be liberated from wrong self-understandings and the constraints of religious legalism and unwieldy denominational structures, so do many of us. Far too often, the stringency and demands of denominationalism or the expectations of previous generations become weights around our necks that hinder us from looking up.

Tradition is the living faith of the dead, whereas traditionalism is the dead faith of the living. Jesus, a radical traditionalist, holds both together. He has come to fulfil the law, but he also calls for new wineskins. His people hold to the unchanging truth of who he is, what he has come to do and how he calls us to live, but they should not domesticate the call of the kingdom.

There is a generation rising around us that is unwilling to be controlled by traditionalism. They will not be held within the confines of what used to be. They are turning away from the nostalgia of the good old days and turning toward what might happen now, or next. They need to know the difference between tradition, which is good, and traditionalism. Many Christians are straining at the leash to try new things, to explore new ways of doing and being the church. While some have fallen into the trap of lazy deconstructionism, many are simply longing for a new wineskin. Those of us who have been entrusted with leadership in God's church during this season must remember that we are ambassadors for the kingdom. We must give people a chance. We must open new spaces, try new ways of being, explore new routes.

I have been an Elim minister for many years, but have also had the privilege of serving in other denominations while retaining my Elim credentials. In all of my pastorates, I have been an advocate for egalitarianism. I consider one of the most important aspects of my long-term ministry to be the teaching of the equality of women and men in terms of what God might call them to and where God might ask them to go. Elim began as an egalitarian movement, then in the 1930s closed its ordination processes to women. It did so because it was seeking respectability in the eyes of the other denominations of the day, not because it had thought through its own theological position on the issue. In the late 1990s the denomination cleared the way for the ordination of women again and began to open its leadership roles to both women and men.

It has been a long and tortuous process for many, but as kingdom people we must not stop. We must continue to champion the belief that what God says about a person is of the utmost importance and that denominational structures should reflect that. We are done with this within our movement. In 2022 we welcomed the first woman on to the national leadership team of the movement, and we lifted the bar on ordination on women in Ireland. I thank God for those changes, but I long to see them progress even more.

Not only that, but we must also work out what it means to raise up new generations of leaders in our churches and in our communities. Our ceiling can be their floor, but for that to happen we must take seriously the call to break open the structures, the systems and the budgets of our churches. I wonder how much money we spend on maintaining what we have rather than investing in what we can become? Jesus' words liberated those who followed him from wrong expectations and control systems within the religious tradition of the day. Surely this is important for us too? What does faithful kingdom living look like for our generation?

Pressing in without pulling down

To be clear, I am not suggesting denominations are wrong, or that it is unfair or unwise for leaders to expect a continued faithfulness to their core beliefs and practices as a particular part of Christ's body – far from it. I delight in being part of the Elim Pentecostal Church and take very seriously the call to honour the convictions of my forebears in the movement of which I am privileged to be part. I have a God-given responsibility to live within the right expectations of my denomination, and I take them very seriously. As recently as our national leadership summit in 2022, our National Director of Ministry, Stuart Blount, reminded the ministers and leaders of the movement that when we are inducted into the pastorate of a local Elim church we are entrusted with the heritage and values of the movement in that place, and it is expected that we will leave an Elim church behind when the time comes for us to vacate that charge. I do, however, believe that we must learn what it is to live in the soil of the kingdom as our primary place of identity and purpose and to allow the specific characteristics of our denominational affiliation to be refracted through the lens of God's kingdom rather than the other way round. We must first and foremost be kingdom people. I think this is happening whether we want it to or not.

The way in which Jesus recasts the understanding of his hearers is remarkable. He does not dismiss the Great Story of the people of God. He enters in and opens a new chapter. The women and men who listen to the Sermon on the Mount are captivated by a radical message that turns their understanding of the world on its head. I believe we need the same thing.

Jesus does not, however, demolish Judaism. He remains faithful to what was but reimagines those parts of it that need to be renewed. He builds out of the history of God's work in the world rather than pulling down that story. Too often, new ideas are seen as automatically being a criticism of what was – that doesn't need to be the case. A new idea can just be a new idea.

Redefining inclusivity

The Sermon on the Mount involves radical reorientation. The excluded, the vulnerable and the forgotten are welcomed in and the lost find a home. But their new identity is never at the expense of a call to the ethical and moral standards of God. The kingdom welcomes the most unexpected of people, but it also brings a call to a radically different life.

The church has much to learn about this in our day and generation. Too often we have hidden behind vacuous statements like 'love the sinner but hate the sin'. We have used such pronouncements as a means of embedding prejudice and enshrining our take on an issue. That must change.

The followers of Jesus who listened to him on that Galilean hillside already knew that the religious establishment did not want them. What they did not know was that God welcomed them. There can be no ambiguity here. God's kingdom has a place for many who cannot find a place in churches. Kingdom people are not all the same colour, they are not all of the same political or theological conviction, and they are not all from the same economic or social class. They do not all speak the same language, and they do not all worship in the same way. Furthermore, they are not primarily defined by their own understanding of their gender or sexuality. If God does not welcome me because I am straight, then it must also be true that God will not reject someone else because they are gay. Yet we cannot simply leave the issue of inclusivity there because the Sermon on the Mount also calls kingdom people into radical obedience.

Jesus' use of the six antitheses in Matthew 5.21–47, and his call that the people of the kingdom should be perfect in Matthew 5.48, are stark reminders that kingdom people are not primarily relativists. We are not free to rewrite the commands and the demands of the Scriptures or of virtue. The King simultaneously invites us into the kingdom and challenges us with the call of a renewed life in the kingdom. Churches and denominations must grapple with this double calling in our own self-understanding. How do we welcome people and hold out for a transformed life? What does it mean to take seriously human identity and human sexuality as set out in the Scriptures? How do we open space to listen to one another across these great cultural and social chasms? How can our churches be safe places for those who want to be in the kingdom and are responding to the call of God while at the same time being communities that hold in the highest regard the ethics and the morals and the holiness of the kingdom?

What do holiness and faithfulness look like?

The Sermon on the Mount is also a manifesto for holiness in all of life. So often, we have allowed the issues of sexuality and gender to become the only issues of moral significance in our churches or in our public debates. A cursory glance at Matthew 5, however, names at least six areas that deserve our attention: how we think about and treat others; our sexual desire and the way we see those to whom we are attracted, relationships and marriage; how we use our words; how we see ourselves in relation to other people, particularly those who think they are better than us and those whom we think we are better than; and how we engage with those we consider to be our enemies. The Sermon challenges us to think about our piety, our attachment to wealth and power, our mental health, how we make judgements and so much more. Its message is broad and sweeping.

I sometimes wonder if we are guilty of spending far too much time arguing and dividing over contentious issues and not nearly enough time discussing the call to virtue, holiness and justice and what it means for us today. Maybe, as kingdom people, we could commit to more time seeing each other and learning from one another and less time pulling one another down and attacking each other. None of that means that we ignore the big issues, but perhaps we need to broaden our understanding of holiness.

I suspect that under all the cultural wars of this present moment there is a deeper wrestle going on. We are not, in the end, arguing over what constitutes a holy and faithful life, although that appears to be the case. We are arguing about what, or who, defines what a holy and faithful life looks like.

Does the culture do that? The Sermon on the Mount shows us that it does not.

Does the teaching of a previous pastor or theologian do that? The Sermon on the Mount shows us that it does not.

Does the prevailing voice of the moment, the popular voice, do that? The Sermon on the Mount shows us that it does not.

Does God do that? The Sermon on the Mount shows us that God does do this – but with one explosive additional caveat. The God who defines us is the God who defines morality and holiness and purity and ethics. This God has given us Scripture as a plumbline against which we measure our own claims of faithfulness and inclusivity and truth and everything else, and Jesus' interpretation of that Scripture is the ultimate seat of authority for us in all of this. Jesus did not contradict Moses – but he went further than his generation had ever heard anyone go before. Matthew does not present Jesus as the King of a kingdom that is defined by Moses or by the long tradition of Judaism. Matthew presents a Jesus who is the defining centre of that kingdom. Everything that went before him, and everything that comes after him, is defined through who he is, what he says and what he has done. The church, as part of the kingdom, must never put itself in the place of the King.

The King defines us. The King is the one who decides who is part of the kingdom and who is not. The King sets the ethical bar for his kingdom. The King is the living, breathing personification of holiness, justice, faithfulness and mercy. The rest of the New Testament, under the inspiration and direction of the Holy Spirit, maps what this means and lays the challenge of it at our feet.

We ignore it at our peril.

Where do we see what it means to be kingdom people at work in the world today?

I want to take you back to the way in which Matthew frames the Sermon on the Mount before setting out a few examples of kingdom people at work in the world today. Remember that Matthew frames the teaching of the Sermon within the context of the authoritative teaching and miraculous ministry of Jesus.[40] Both of these attributes of kingdom people matter, and we will pick this connection up in the next chapter of *Flipped*, but for now, consider with me the following examples of either the power of Jesus' message or the demonstration of Jesus' healing power. I am deliberately choosing examples that most people will not know about because I think we too often run toward big projects or big names to illustrate a message like the one I am sharing here.

Kyria Network[41]

The Kyria Network is committed to championing, empowering and releasing women into spheres of influence. Its CEO, Amy Summerfield, is a local church leader and she is passionate about seeing women affirmed in the church and serving alongside men. The Network is active across all parts of the United Kingdom and is growing in numbers and in influence, but behind it all is the belief that women matter in the church and they cannot simply be ignored or held back.

Kyria wants to champion women by supporting female leaders and advocating for cultural change and a biblical perspective that releases them fully. It wants to empower women by developing a network of encouragement, belonging and strength that empowers women of influence. It wants to equip women and churches so that women are released to lead effectively in every sphere of society. The network has a resource known as The Well, which offers books, blogs, videos, podcasts and websites that will encourage and equip leaders. It also offers support to authors, teachers and speakers who want to pave the way for women in leadership.

This kind of initiative makes a space for people who are currently not at the table and invites others to do the same. It is not a denominational initiative, although it is supported by a number of denominations. It isn't big budget, but it is high impact. Amy and the team have heard the call of God in their own lives, and they are seeking to create space for others to discover the value, purpose and significance of women in ministry. Kyria isn't doing what it is doing because it is popular or easy; rather, it is doing what it does because it knows that it is right.

Alabaster

Taking its name from the story of the women who anointed Jesus,[42] Alabaster is a new ministry in Northern Ireland that is seeking to gather young adults together in worship and devotion to Jesus. It is so new and so small that, at the time of writing, it does not have any budget or a website.

Facilitated by Anna and Jacob Arnold, the community meets regularly in a local barn to pray, to worship and to sit at the feet of Jesus. It has captured something of the connection between devotion and behaviour that is recorded in Matthew 6, and it wants to help others to find their identity, worth and value in the intimacy and acceptance that Jesus offers. Its members know that new initiatives and projects will probably flow from their gatherings, but they neither want to predict what they might be nor control how they might develop. Their times together are times of sung worship, but also times of encounter, where God is moving in power, healing and restoring lives. God is at work as Jesus is being uplifted.

Laura[43]

Laura is gay. I was the first person she told. She sat with me in my study one afternoon and unpacked her story. She has always experienced an attraction to people of the same sex, but she has never felt that she could tell anyone. She loves the church that she is part of, but she is not sure how they will respond when (not if) they find out. She hasn't told her whole family yet. She came to see me because she felt safe and because she said she knew I would not judge her harshly. She also knows that I have a conservative theological stance on issues relating to human sexuality.

When she told me, I thanked her for her honesty and we wept together. She told me that church should be the community where she feels able to be her most honest self, but it is often the community where she must hide a significant part of who she is. I am in no doubt whatsoever that Laura is a child of God and that she is in God's kingdom.

My journey with her is the same as the journey I have made, and am making, with dozens of others. We meet, we pray and we read the Bible together. I help her to understand the different approaches that different churches take to the issues of human sexuality and I help her to work out where she places herself on the issue.

I never tell her what to think and I never tell her what to do. That is not my role in this relationship. She has asked my what my position on the issue is, and I have explained it to her. She has asked what my church's position is, and that of my denomination, on the issue of human sexuality, and I have explained those to her too. I am committed to walking with Laura for as long as she wants me to, and I am determined to help her to pray through the choices and decisions that lie before her. Those decisions will then shape the church she is part of and the way in which she lives her life before God.

Above all, I want her to know that God sees her, welcomes her and will not walk away from her. At no point have I, or will I, water down my understanding of the Scriptures on the issues she faces. Nor am I passive in the relationship – I pray earnestly for her and the many others with whom I walk in these sorts of situations.

What is my prayer? That they will discover the life of the kingdom and the welcome of the King. That they will know that they are seen and loved and known. That they will hear the voice of God through the text of God's word, the example of God's Son and the whisper of God's Spirit and that they will be obedient to the call that God places on their lives.

I don't pray that they will agree with me, because my job is not to define them but to love them. I don't pray that they will come to my church. I pray that they will find the place where their conscience, their reading of Scripture and their experience of God are united. I have found that place in my fellowship, my denomination and my life, and I know the joy that it brings. I do not judge Laura; I love her, tell her the truth as best I can and I walk with her as she figures out what her life of obedience will look like.

Moot[44]

Situated in the very heart of London, in one of the capital's oldest and narrowest streets, is St Mary Aldermary, next to modern office buildings and located on the ancient Roman road of Watling Street, in the City. Generations of Londoners have passed its walls since it was founded by Benedictine Monks in around the twelfth century.

The most recent church building, built in 1682, offers sanctuary under the name of Moot to busy city workers, weary tourists and those who need to discover and express Christianity in a new way. The space is used as a church, offering monastic-style morning and evening prayer, Eucharist, meditation, Taizé yoga and a space for those who want to explore and deepen their faith. Alongside the practising church is Host, a café that operates in the beautiful interior, so those who are not practising Christians can still grab a directly traded coffee or a cake and witness Christian worship in action.

The ordained vicar is supported by a team of workers and volunteers, such as Café Coordinator and Mission and Evangelism worker, Vanessa Elston, who explains:

This is a very sacred space, yet people want to know if we are a coffee shop or a church, and are taken aback when they realise that we are both. Host is open to people of all ages and from all walks of life, and that unlike other coffee houses, we do not insist on people buying coffee to stay here, so we are opening up the church as a public 'third space' and for everyone – all day and every day.[45]

Moot has been in existence for 11 years and a new-monastic community for six years, while offering hospitality with Host for the last two years. The café has been a focal point for those who are not normal faith seekers and offers a sanctuary amid the noisy, bustling streets of the city. Its 'Rhythm of Life' engages with the question, how should we live while on the pilgrim route, while challenging consumerism, individualism, greed and the cult of celebrity? Living the Rhythm through prayer and worship enables community members to discern right ways of living, and right responses to the challenges that we all face in modern culture and in ourselves.

It is this Rhythm of Life that has enabled Moot to connect with busy executives and city workers. Many who have no church background come to the weekly Wednesday evening meditation group as a space where they can experience stillness and silence with others. Workers have opened up about how dehumanizing the city work culture can be, stating that the church provides a unique space where they can openly express themselves. Vanessa suggests:

The world is looking for integrity. At Moot we seek to be open and honest about our own journey, how we haven't got it all together, how we are novices, very much beginners in practices like meditation and contemplation, and others are attracted to this. We are not trying to push people to God, but help them realise that God is present in their lives and we simply help them discover God working through them.[46]

While operating the church like an 'open sitting-room' and a space where 'people are known', Moot is helping unemployed volunteers find work experience and employment in a highly competitive part of the world. The team has helped two unemployed volunteers into full-time work, and Host is currently setting up work experience placements for women from the Marylebone Project, a Church Army Hostel for homeless women.

Moot has also supported and inspired others in their creativity, offering residencies and exhibition space to artists and facilitating lunchtime performances for musicians. Vocalist Georgina Brett recently performed her medieval-style piece 'Leanate', using her voice and effects pedals to create an instant choir. Music is a way for many to experience a deeper connection with God, in a space that's unapologetically Christian.

Others have expressed their relationships with God in different ways. Since operating at St Mary Aldermary, Moot has become a 'vocational factory'. With 90 people on the electoral roll, one member is training in the priesthood, five are in discernment for a vocation and one is a pioneering minister.

This is a safe community, but a challenging one, where people are seen and heard and a space is created for them to discover the grace and mercy of God for themselves.

What if all of our churches were like that?

Let's pray

Father,

Too often we have allowed ourselves to be constrained by the expectations and definitions of others. Forgive them for making such demands of us, and forgive us for yielding to them.

So often, we live our lives upside down, valuing the wrong things, wanting to be seen with those whom we think are the right people and making the wrong choices. Give us grace to find our identity, worth and purpose in you and not in the things that we have, the people that we know or the status that others afford us.

Help us to remember your call on our lives and to live in the light of your commands. May others see Christ in us.

Help us to grow spiritually. Draw us into the cycle of your life and root us in your grace. Help us to understand that your grace is not a licence to do what we want but the power from which we can live as you designed. Enable us to take your call to holiness and faithfulness seriously, and forgive us when we turn it into a pale reflection of our culture's accepted norms.

Help us to be careful with our emotions.

Help us to be honest about our desires and never to objectify another human being.

Help us to treasure our relationships and families.

Help us to be true to our word.

Help us to have a right estimation of ourselves, and forgive us when we see ourselves as better or worse than you have made us.

Help us to love those who hurt us.

Deepen our faith, strengthen our devotion and connect our inner world to our outer choices.

Enable us to lay our anxieties at your feet and to trust you for tomorrow.

Give us grace to be kind and compassionate in our judgements.

We cannot do any of this without the power of your Spirit, so we pray for the continual filling of the Spirit's power in our lives and presence in our days.

May we choose the right thing, not the easy thing.

May we grow and mature, and may our lives bear witness to our faith.

May we live under your lordship and walk in friendship with you always.

May the storms and challenges of our lives become moments when our faith is strengthened and our resolve deepened.

Help us to see ourselves as you see us, and to see others as you see them.

May our lives be welcoming places for all whom you send to us.

Amen.

3

The purpose of the kingdom

The world says, 'Keep all you can.'
Jesus says, 'Give all you have.'

As you go, proclaim the good news, 'The kingdom of heaven
has come near.' Cure the sick, raise the dead, cleanse the
lepers, cast out demons.
(Matthew 10.7–8)

Man (*sic*) is to labor to take the raw materials of the earth and
remodel it according to the heavenly blueprint . . . Heaven
forms the model for earth – socially, morally, spiritually, and
in every other way.[1]

I first met Jackie Pullinger in the late 1990s. Her incredible life is
littered with accounts of God's grace at work, God's provision being
released and God's guidance being followed.[2] She is one of the most
remarkable leaders of the twentieth century and I am sure that, in
years to come, much more will emerge into the public eye about her
courage, conviction and determination.

On this occasion, our meeting was in a house in Hampshire.
Jackie was back from Hong Kong on furlough and we were having
coffee together. After chatting about how she had navigated the
death of her husband and how things were going in Hong Kong
and in China, we began to talk about legacy and planning. She
dismissed any sense of planning for the future, believing that if God
had called her and brought her to Hong Kong against all the odds
and despite serious setbacks and opposition, then God could raise

up someone else to take on the work. She was not in the least bit concerned about legacy.

We then started to talk about what she did and why she did it. Her answers were crystal clear and laser focused. She went to Hong Kong because God had told her to go and advance the kingdom of heaven among those whom the world had forgotten. She had no other purpose when she went, and she had no other intention at the time of our meeting. She considers herself an ambassador for the kingdom and a servant of the King. She believes her life is entirely devoted to this purpose alone. Matthew's record of Jesus' commissioning of the disciples would suggest that Jackie is right.

Jesus clearly announced his intention to Peter to build the church, but he also gave Peter further instruction:

> I will build my church, and the gates of Hades will not prevail against it. I will give you the keys of the kingdom of heaven, and whatever you bind on earth will be bound in heaven, and whatever you loose on earth will be loosed in heaven.
> (Matthew 16.18–19)

It is not our job to build the church – that is the job of Jesus. It is, however, our job to partner with Jesus in the building of his church and in the advancement of his kingdom. It was this call, to advance the kingdom, that sent Jackie Pullinger to Hong Kong, and it is this call that has kept her there. It is also this call that I heard when I was converted in 1986 and has kept me committed to the local church and to preaching, teaching, leading and pastoring for almost 34 years at the time of writing. I pray that I will be obedient to that call until the day I die.

Jesus' words to Peter make it clear that Jesus will build his church, but what are the 'keys to the kingdom' that Jesus makes mention of in this passage? I want to explore some of the possible answers to that question. To do so, we will consider three central passages in Matthew's gospel – Matthew 16.13–20, Matthew 10.5–15 and Matthew 28.16–20. Matthew 16 deals with the foundation of the church and the keys of the kingdom; Matthew 10 deals with the commissioning of the disciples and Matthew 28 deals with the commissioning of all who claim to be followers of Christ. As we explore these texts, we will see again the upside-down nature of the kingdom of heaven that requires us to adjust our thinking. Doing so ensures that we build on Christ's foundational purpose of the kingdom.

I want to explore just one foundation, and one purpose.

The foundation: remaining true to Peter's faithful confession of Christ

Now when Jesus came into the district of Caesarea Philippi, he asked his disciples, 'Who do people say that the Son of Man is?' And they said, 'Some say John the Baptist, but others Elijah, and still others Jeremiah or one of the prophets.' He said to them, 'But who do you say that I am?' Simon Peter answered, 'You are the Messiah, the Son of the living God.' And Jesus answered him, 'Blessed are you, Simon son of Jonah! For flesh and blood has not revealed this to you, but my Father in heaven. And I tell you, you are Peter, and on this rock I will build my church, and the gates of Hades will not prevail against it. I will give you the keys of the kingdom of heaven, and whatever you bind on earth will be bound in heaven, and whatever you loose on earth will be loosed in heaven.' Then he sternly ordered the disciples not to tell anyone that he was the Messiah.

(Matthew 16.13–20)

This exchange between Jesus and his disciples took place in Caesarea Philippi, a Gentile town deeply linked to Pan,[3] not far from the source of the Jordan River and about 25 miles north of the Sea of Galilee.[4] It is almost certainly an area that was marked by a great geological chasm or ravine, which was believed to be a gateway to Hades.[5] It is deeply significant that it was here that Jesus reminded his disciples that his kingdom has the power to confront the forces of evil and to push them back in the certainty of ultimate victory. It was also here that he set out the foundation of his kingdom. It is not surprising, therefore, that this passage is among the most contested in the New Testament because, if we can contest the foundations of the kingdom, then the building that is placed upon those foundations is more likely to collapse. To understand the dispute, we must first see the text.

In reading Matthew's outline of the event (vv. 16–20), we are listening in to a conversation between Jesus and his disciples (principally Peter) (vv. 13b–19), which is framed by Matthew's introduction (v. 13) and conclusion (v. 20). In the dialogue, we discover that Jesus asks two questions (vv. 13, 15), and then responds to Peter's confession, (vv. 17–19).[6] The two questions and their responses are not disputed, nor is the beginning of Jesus's response to Peter's confession.

- **Question 1 (asked of the disciples):** Who do people say that the Son of Man is? (v. 13).
  Answer (from the disciples): John the Baptist, Elijah, Jeremiah or one of the prophets (v. 14).
- **Question 2 (asked of the disciples):** But who do you say that I am? (v. 15).
  Answer (from Simon Peter): You are the Messiah, the Son of the living God (v. 16).
- **The beginning of Jesus' response to Peter's confession:** Simon is blessed; Simon's insight about the identity of Jesus has been given to Simon by God the Father (v. 17); Simon has also been given a new name – Peter (v. 18a).

It is the next part of the dialogue that has generated much disagreement.

> And I tell you, you are Peter, and on this rock I will build my church, and the gates of Hades will not prevail against it. I will give you the keys of the kingdom of heaven, and whatever you bind on earth will be bound in heaven, and whatever you loose on earth will be loosed in heaven.' Then he sternly ordered the disciples not to tell anyone that he was the Messiah.
> (Matthew 16.18–19)

What is the rock upon which Christ will build his church? Is it Peter in his natural state, making him the first pope and elevating his role, and therefore all who occupy that role after him because 'the pope is crowned with a triple crown, as king of heaven, of earth and of hell',[7] bearing a temporal and a spiritual sword? This is the basis of Roman Catholic teaching and leads to the conviction that Peter and his successors hold:

> the first place of honour and jurisdiction in the government of his whole church . . . Consequently, to be true followers of Christ all Christians, both among the clergy and the laity, must be in communion with the See of Rome, where Peter rules in the person of his successor.[8]

Is it the confession of Christ as the Messiah and the Son of God that is the foundation stone of the kingdom?[9] Is it the apostolic confession of who Christ is, revealed to Peter by the Holy Spirit, thus making Peter representative of a faithful understanding and transmission of the Person of Jesus? What if all three have some merit?

The foundation of the kingdom is, first and foremost, Christ – the Messiah and the Son of the Living God. This reality can only be grasped by the power of the Holy Spirit and the revelation of

God. It is a truth that was first transmitted to an ordinary man called Cephas, who became known as Peter, and then to the other faithful apostles. They and their confession are key in the kingdom of heaven because Christ is both the King of the kingdom and its cornerstone. If he is not at the heart of the kingdom, then there is no kingdom to speak of. He is the one to whom the apostles pointed,[10] and he is still the beating heart of the kingdom because where there is no King, there is no kingdom.

It does not matter how much we use the word 'Christian' to describe what we do or who we are. The profound challenge of this first principle is that if we do not build on the *faithful* revelation of who Christ is, then we are not building *his* kingdom. I do not mean that we are confined and constrained by a Jesus who fits our theological formulae, or is a pale reflection of the Christ of Scripture. We have had quite enough of that. Too often the quest for the historical Jesus has left us bereft of his passion, compassion and power. Nor do I mean that we allow Jesus to become a pale reflection of the most recent sociological or cultural idea. There has been quite enough talk of a hidden Jesus, or a concealed Jesus, who stalks the pages of the New Testament like a phantom – or, worse still, deliberately hides from us to confuse us.

I am arguing that we let the Jesus of the New Testament be the Jesus who sits enthroned at the centre of our lives and of the church. This Jesus – the Messiah, the Son of the Living God – is the one who pulls down strongholds, rescues the perishing and lifts the broken. He challenges us with his compassion and his inclusivity, he confronts us with his call to holiness, he draws us in with his beauty and he leaves us speechless at his power and authority.

The exchange between Jesus and the disciples at Caesarea Philippi is a salutary reminder that we must be careful not to create Jesus in our own image. While some may call him a prophet and some may give him special status, in the upside-down kingdom he is the Messiah. We are building his kingdom only insofar as we are faithful to him as we discover him in the Scriptures. The confession of who he is was revealed to Peter and the other apostles, and then to Paul,[11] and then to the next generation and then to the next . . . until eventually it reached us. Now we must remain *faithful* to this Jesus and ensure that we pass the baton to the next generation, and then to the next, and so on and so on until the day when Christ returns. It is this sense of receiving the *apostolic* gospel that is found in Paul's words to the Corinthians and in his words to the young pastor in Ephesus, Timothy.

> Now I should remind you, brothers and sisters, of the good news that I proclaimed to you, which you in turn received, in which also you stand, through which also you are being saved, if you hold firmly to the message that I proclaimed to you – unless you have come to believe in vain.
> For I handed on to you as of first importance what I in turn had received: that Christ died for our sins in accordance with the scriptures, and that he was buried, and that he was raised on the third day in accordance with the scriptures, and that he appeared to Cephas, then to the twelve.
> (1 Corinthians 15.1–5)

> You then, my child, be strong in the grace that is in Christ Jesus; and what you have heard from me through many witnesses entrust to faithful people who will be able to teach others as well.
> (2 Timothy 2.1–2)

If staying in allegiance to a faithful identification of Christ is a foundation of the kingdom's purpose, then following his instructions is a fundamental outworking of that faithful confession. There are few places that provide a better summary of those instructions than Matthew 10 and Matthew 28.

The purpose: as kingdom people, we are called to continue the ministry of Jesus

Then Jesus summoned his twelve disciples and gave them authority over unclean spirits, to cast them out, and to cure every disease and every sickness . . . 'As you go, proclaim the good news, "The kingdom of heaven has come near." Cure the sick, raise the dead, cleanse the lepers, cast out demons.'
(Matthew 10.1, 7–8)

And Jesus came to them and said, 'All authority in heaven and earth has been given to me. Go therefore and make disciples of all nations, baptizing them in the name of the Father and of the Son and of the Holy Spirit, and teaching them to obey everything that I have commanded you. And remember, I am with you always, to the end of the age'.
(Matthew 28.18–20)

These two passages carry with them some of the most clearly distilled instructions around our purposes as the followers of King Jesus that can be found in the New Testament. The first, Matthew 10, is given to the disciples in relation to their ministry within Israel and to the Jews. The second, Matthew 28, extends that ministry to the world, or to 'all nations'.[12] Both carry the sense that what Jesus is telling his followers to do is to be a way of life, not just an activity or a project list – hence the phrases, 'As you go,' and, 'Go,' the latter being the same kind of instruction as the former. These combined imperatives give the sense of urgency, intentionality and focus.

It is important to note, though, that both passages also carry a clear reminder that we go in the authority of Christ, not in our own authority. Christ entrusts us with his power and authority, and he sends us in his power and authority to carry out his mission. There is a sense in which we do not have ministries of our own. We are his messengers, his servants and his subjects. We are citizens of his kingdom. He goes with us, he guides us and we are reminded that our purposes must fit with his commands, not the other way round.

In an age of self-determination and individualism, there are few things more countercultural than this call to lay our lives at another's feet. We give up our rights in this kingdom for the King,[13] learning to live as if our old lives have gone and new lives have come[14] because we are new creations,[15] crucified with Christ, and he now lives in us.[16] Christ's purpose is now our purpose,[17] and what pleases him and fulfils his mission is now the determining factor in our lives.

The combined impact of Jesus' instructions to his disciples in Matthew 10 and Matthew 28 reveal three key ways in which we continue the ministry and message of Jesus.

Priority one: we announce the kingdom

Jesus is clear that his followers must 'proclaim' the good news.[18] This urgent aspect of kingdom life is expressed through the use of a strong Greek word, κηρύσσω (kērussō), which carries a sense of announcement, urgency and persuasion to accept the message being spoken.[19] It is the word that Matthew chooses to use to describe John the Baptist's preaching[20] and the preaching of Jesus,[21] and it is Matthew's word of choice when it comes to expressing the reality of the kingdom of heaven in words.[22] This sense of urgent announcement and pleading, which we often describe as preaching, characterized the life of the early church.[23] Later, for Paul, it would be the word that he would use to define his core understanding of how the message of the kingdom was conveyed and his own sense of vocation.[24] It is the word that Peter uses to describe Christ's ministry between Christ's death and resurrection,[25] and the word that John uses to describe the way in which the angel announced the Lamb in John's heavenly vision.[26]

In a world that has become inoculated to the power of words because of their overuse, the idea of preaching and proclamation being at the heart of the purpose of the kingdom has been criticized and minimized. It is suggested that we should preach the kingdom in our actions and only use words if they are needed. It is even suggested that this has been the teaching of previous generations of saints such as Saint Francis of Assisi.[27] The problem is that Christ has made it clear that words are a vital part of our kingdom purpose. While we must ensure that our lives do not contradict our message, lest we be guilty of hypocrisy, we must equally ensure that we use words to explain the kingdom and to announce it. The New Testament is crystal clear about this – whether we be initiating the dialogue or announcement or responding to others' questions:

> But how are they to call on one in whom they have not believed? And how are they to believe in one of whom they have never heard? And how are they to hear without some to proclaim him? And how are they to proclaim him unless they are sent?
> (Romans 10.14–15)

> Always be ready to make your defence to anyone who demands from you an account of the hope that is in you; yet do it with gentleness and reverence.
> (1 Peter 3.15–16)

Jesus' command to his followers is that they must do exactly what he did – *announce* the kingdom. But there is more to this injunction – it is the *good news* that we proclaim. Our announcement does not shy away from the issues of sin, shame, failure and the need to repent – after all, this was the basis of Jesus' own proclamation of the kingdom, a point emphasized by the way in which Matthew reveals to us the first public words of Christ's own ministry:

From that time Jesus began to proclaim, 'Repent, for the kingdom of heaven has come near.'
(Matthew 4.17)

Our words continue to matter. Our cultures, our communities and our churches(!) need us to articulate the hope and the beauty of the kingdom with our words. Far from being less important than in previous generations, our preaching, teaching and discipleship are more important now than they have ever been. The challenge is for us to hold together, in our words and our proclamation, the full beauty of the kingdom message. It includes the reality that God has dealt with sin in Christ, bearing our guilt, carrying our shame and taking upon himself the punishment that we deserved. This is what makes hope possible – and the message of a hope that is possible and purpose that can be transformative is good news!

The *good news* of the kingdom is that change is possible, God has come near, a rescuer has come! We are not trapped in the endless cycle of failure, shame and disgrace. We are not locked out from the purposes of heaven and the joy of living as God intended. A better life, a liberated life and a transformed life are all possible because of who Jesus is and what Jesus did, from beginning to end. His birth, life, death and resurrection are all vital components of the kingdom message, as are the giving of the Spirit, Christ's continual intercession and his promised return.

Jesus changes everything because in Christ God was reconciling the world to himself.[28] He is the cipher for genuine human flourishing. No wonder, then, that he not only announces the kingdom, but also demonstrates it and calls us to do the same.

Priority two: we demonstrate the kingdom

The second part of Jesus' instruction to the disciples in Matthew 10 is that they are to show the communities around them what God's kingdom looks like – they are to evidence its reality.

> Cure the sick, raise the dead, cleanse the lepers, cast out demons.
> (Matthew 10.8)

It is not surprising that Jesus instructs his disciples to do this, since these activities sat at the very heart of his own ministry.[29] In fact, when he announced the heartbeat of his ministry, he boldly proclaimed that he had come to demonstrate the power of God in the world by reading from the prophet Isaiah, stating that the words of liberation and promises of freedom had begun to be fulfilled *in him*.[30] There are two ways in which we should consider these words, the first of which is literally.

We must be careful not to move to allegorizing the demonstrations of the kingdom that Jesus sets out in Matthew 10. We are far too ready to jump to the wider application of these words without first seeing that they were a call to see the miraculous intervention of God in a broken and pained world. Jesus sends his followers to cure the sick, to raise the dead, to cleanse the lepers and to cast out demons *literally*. The miraculous intervention of God in the world through the ministry of Jesus, and then through the ministry of his disciples, was vital evidence that the kingdom had come. It still is.

Just as in the gospel of John, where the miracles of Jesus are described as *signs* that point to who Jesus is and what he does,[31] so in the world today the miraculous intervention of God continues to point to who God is and what God does and to what God's kingdom looks like. It strikes me that this is one of the *flipped* aspects of God's kingdom in our minority world in the Northern Hemisphere that we must take more seriously. With all of our cultural advancement and intellectual prowess, it is easy for us to dismiss the miraculous as belonging to a bygone era, or as somehow primitive. It may have been foundational, but it is no longer required. We have moved beyond it. Nothing could be further from the truth. We continue to be in desperate need of God's direct, clear and miraculous intervention in our world. Not only is that the case, but the mission of the people of God, as kingdom signposts, is to show that God is still in the world and that God is still at work.

In my own travels around the world, I have seen the hunger for the miraculous intervention of God so many times. From the streets of Mumbai in India to the townships of Zimbabwe; from the communities of El Salvador to the villages of Thailand I have witnessed God's kingdom coming in miraculous healing, resurrection power, deliverance of people from demons and the inclusion of those who have been outcast. These miraculous realities can also be seen in the countries and communities of Europe and North America, though. It is not true to suggest that these miraculous interventions of God only belong in other places. I have witnessed God move in miraculous power right across the United Kingdom, Continental Europe and the United States of America.

My own church tradition is the Pentecostal stream, and in it we regularly pray for the sick and seek the miraculous intervention of God in the lives of women and men. We need this more than we have ever needed it, and we are called to demonstrate this purpose of the kingdom as much now as we have ever been.

The second way in which we can read these words is to understand the broad categories of what Jesus is instructing his disciples to do. He is sending them to be compassionate healers and to be involved in the care of the sick, the care of the dying, the care of those who have been ostracized by their societies and the care of those who have fallen foul of evil forces and power. This is the call of Christ to us, his people, to be involved in the pain and the heartbreak of our communities as harbingers of hope. As kingdom people, we bring hope and healing with us. We not only *announce* it; we also live it out. The call of Matthew 10 is a call to involvement in our world, a call to engagement in issues of justice, advocacy and action. We are not those who stand on the edge of our communities shouting at them. We are those who are involved in our communities, at the coalface of injustice, chiselling at the granite faces of prejudices, racism, isolation, poverty and exclusion and standing for the marginalized, the poor and the forgotten.

These commitments can be seen in churches, charities and organizations up and down the United Kingdom and around the world. They can also be seen in the daily lives of Christians who are simply going to work and doing their jobs as teachers, nurses, car mechanics, politicians, businesswomen, lecturers, accountants and carers. Wherever followers of Christ can be found, we are called to be people who demonstrate the kingdom, not just talk about it. In the words of the Apostle James, speaking specifically in relation to the poor:

> Every generous act of giving, with every perfect gift, is from above, coming down from the Father of lights, with whom there is no variation or shadow due to change . . .
> Religion that is pure and undefiled before God, the Father, is this: to care for orphans and widows in their distress, and to keep oneself unstained by the world . . .
> Show me your faith without works, and I by my works will show you my faith.
> (James 1.17, 27; 2.18)

In Matthew's gospel, Jesus tells us that when we come face to face with him, he will speak of our care for the marginalized, excluded, sick, imprisoned, naked and poor.[32] We are called both to speak of the kingdom and to demonstrate it. To remove either of these imperatives is to remove our effectiveness in the world.

Priority three: we make disciples of Jesus who live for the kingdom

Third, and this time from Matthew 28, known as the Great Commission, we are called to make disciples. There are three main words used in the New Testament to describe what a disciple is. One, the most prevalent, is related to the idea of an apprentice who learns on the job. A second carries the idea of a mimic. The third brings with it a commitment to being a student. All three meanings are involved in Jesus' call upon his people to make disciples. In the Great Commission, Jesus unpacks what it means to make disciples – it involves enabling people to identify with Christ and his church through baptism (which points to the need for new birth into God's kingdom), and it involves teaching people to live faithfully in Christ and for Christ.

The call to make disciples who make disciples sits at the heart of the purpose of the kingdom. We are never called to simply make converts, or to convince people to pray a simple prayer of conversion. We cannot make Christians. We cannot force people into God's kingdom and we must not narrow our vocation down to simply getting people to come to church. Rather, it is the task of kingdom people to ensure that those who come to Christ are well birthed, enabled to follow Christ and live in Christ's purposes and plans for them and for the world. We are not primarily called to make people nice, to make them good or to make them pleasant. We are called to make disciples.

Disciples are mimics – they live like Jesus; they are students – they take his teaching and instruction seriously; and they are apprentices – they walk with him and learn from him how to truly live.[33] It is, without question, the great task of pastors and teachers in God's church to make disciples. This is the call that sits at the heart of Jesus' expectation of *every* local church *everywhere*. It is not an optional extra, or a bolt-on for the privileged few. It is the central call of Christ upon his people so that his kingdom can continue to be extended and demonstrated to the world. We are disciples who make disciples, but we must ensure that the disciples that we are forming are birthed with the right purpose and built on the right foundation. That foundation is the confession of Christ as Messiah, the Son of God, and that purpose is proclaiming the good news of the kingdom in everything we do and in everything we are.

The call to build on the faithful apostolic confession of Christ and to ensure that we stay aligned to kingdom principles by preaching the kingdom, demonstrating the kingdom and making disciples of Jesus are hard work. They take a lifetime of dedication and commitment. Although we can see sudden and rapid growth, these purposes are normally birthed slowly, which is why Matthew portrays Jesus as using images of yeast, light, salt, mustard seeds and small things in his kingdom parables across his gospel.[34] In a world where we want instant answers, and in church cultures that so often prize the big above the small and the glitzy above the mundane, charisma above character and popularity above faithfulness, we would do well to remember that this foundation and this purpose are two of the most contested things in the call of the church as an embassy of the kingdom. But here is the challenge.

Whatever else we might do, if our churches and our understanding of Christianity are not built upon a faithful confession of Christ and given to his kingdom purposes, then we are not agents of the kingdom. The world is not changed by denominations or Christian empires or Christian megastars or trendy notions of what being a Christian means. The world is changed by women and men who are called to confess Christ, to take up their cross and to follow him.

Let's pray
Giver of Purpose and Life,
Help us to lay our lives at your feet for the purposes of your kingdom.
Forgive us when we replace the centrality of your Son with the centrality of our own ideas.
Forgive us when we build with wood, hay and stubble that will be

burned up under pressure and blown away by the winds of adversity instead of with the silver and gold of your call upon our lives.

Help us to put your call upon us first.

Help us to shape everything we are and everything we do by your call to proclaim your kingdom and to demonstrate its power.

We give you our words, our thoughts, our hearts, our wills, our homes, our lives, our careers, our choices, our families and our longings.

We lay everything we are at your feet and ask that you will use it for your glory.

As we think about the people and situations in our lives today, we pray that you will show us how to live so that you will be seen in everything we are and everything we do.

Help us to put you first and to be kingdom people before we are anything else.

Amen.

4

The perspective of the kingdom

The world says, 'Worry about tomorrow.'
Jesus says, 'Trust God today.'

The Sermon on the Mount has been described in so many ways. Perhaps the image of looking down a microscope at a single grain of sand is also helpful. Despite the beauty of that single grain when magnified by the microscope's lens, it is only a tiny speck of what we can see when compared with the beauty of the fuller picture of famous beaches such as Porthcurno in Cornwall or Saunton Sands in Devon. The Sermon on the Mount is like a heavenly grain of sand that points to the beauty of the kingdom.

Matthew teaches us how to see things in the way God really sees them. The world says, 'Worry about tomorrow.' Jesus says, 'Trust God today.' In the kingdom of God, truth, honesty, faithfulness, accountability, unity, community and faith all matter. And if we live our lives in this way, as citizens of heaven, both when scattered and gathered, then this can be a powerful witness to God's reign and rule.

Ruth Graham

The famed evangelist Billy Graham, remembered for his straight-forward sharing of the gospel, died aged 99 on 21 February 2018. Like many people, I set time aside to watch the funeral online, being unable to get to the service. More than 2,000 guests attended his funeral in a large tent, like the tent missions he used to preach in his home town of Charlotte, North Carolina. Christian leaders from more than 50 countries attended, alongside the then US

President Donald Trump and Vice President Mike Pence. Billy Graham had planned the funeral himself more than a decade before his death.

There were tributes from a range of people. Billy Graham's five children spoke at the funeral. What struck me the most was the testimony of Ruth Graham, who spoke about her father's forgiveness.

Ruth's marriage ended in divorce after 21 years. She moved away and made a fresh start near her sister. The pastor of her new church introduced her to a handsome widower. Both her mother and her father rang her and suggested Ruth take things a little more slowly, but Ruth married him. Within 24 hours of the wedding, she knew she had made a mistake. Five weeks later she fled home as she was afraid of him. She drove for two days, worried about what her family would say. She drove round the last bend toward her parents' house and saw her dad waiting for her. He wrapped his arms around her and said, 'Welcome home.'

He showed her what God is like that day. Billy Graham was the same in public as he was in private. He had a kingdom perspective. A powerful witness in the public and private arena.

Manna 4 Many[1]

Between January and June 2022, more than 40 people died on the streets of Belfast because of a bad batch of drugs. One of the many charities that is working hard to try to make a difference is Manna 4 Many.

Stanley Donaghy, the founder of the charity, is an ordinary working-class man from Belfast. He felt the nudge of God to do something because he recognized the needs of the homeless in Northern Ireland's capital city some years ago. Over time, he has converted old Post Office delivery trolleys to delivery stations and adapted a van and a couple of buses. He has a small team of volunteers who help, and they run a charity shop to support the ministry. The team is on the streets of Belfast every Thursday night, serving food and hot drinks, offering prayer and support, enabling street sleepers to get a shower or to access help. They regularly lead people into a relationship with Jesus and they function with almost no budget. They are entirely dependent upon the donations and the help of individuals. Very few churches help them with the work, and the volunteers come from a range of denominational backgrounds.

The individuals who serve through Manna 4 Many see the beauty and dignity of every single person that they meet. While officials in various statutory agencies are debating and discussing how to tackle the homeless and drug challenges Belfast faces, this team is committed to living out the call of Jesus to serve the broken and to love the unseen and unnoticed people of the city. They see the people in front of them as God sees them.

God perspective: how God sees us and how we see ourselves

In Matthew 5, Jesus helps his listeners to understand who they are in the eyes of God and how this affects the way they see themselves and their place in the world. He does so by offering them a new perspective on their own worth and their circumstances[2] and by reminding them of their vocation.[3] Once he has done this, he confronts them with the righteous and holy demands of God, which he has come to fulfil, reminding them that there is a way of living that far outstrips anything that they have seen thus far and which is all-demanding in its pervasiveness and power.[4] He then defines for them what a liberated life actually looks like, re-emphasizing the connection between their private, hidden lives and their public lives.[5] Lastly, he makes crystal clear the call of God upon them in one short, challenging and unforgettable statement.[6]

The Beatitudes: a new perspective on personal worth and circumstances[7]

An invitation to a flipped perspective on their lives

There are eight blessings in Matthew 5.3–10 which are so counter-cultural that they would be considered offensive if they were not true. In verse 11, we see an additional blessing, but I think it should be seen as slightly different in nature from the others, and I'll explain why in due course.

Each beatitude begins with a Greek word that is translated into English as 'blessed' or 'happy' or something similar. The Greek word is μακάριος (makario) and is very strong in its message.[8] The word carries a sense of abundant joy and gratefulness, almost a sense of unbridled delight. That's hard to understand when you read what Jesus is actually saying in the Beatitudes. He tells his listeners that they are to be overjoyed in their poverty of spirit;[9] overjoyed in their mourning;[10] overjoyed in their meekness;[11] overjoyed in their hunger and thirst for righteousness;[12] overjoyed when they show mercy;[13] overjoyed when they are pure in heart;[14] overjoyed when they are peacemakers[15] and overjoyed when they are persecuted for righteousness' sake.[16]

On the surface, it seems impossibly unfair to suggest that those who are poor or poor in spirit should be ecstatically happy, or that those who are mourning can simultaneously be brimming over with unbridled joy. It doesn't make sense in isolation from the rest of the gospel of Matthew. But it does make sense when you put these words into context. In fact, when we see the words in context, we see just how upside down these principles are.

There are three things to consider. First, Matthew is speaking to a group of people who are almost certainly poor, excluded and considered unimportant in Jewish society. Remember the context of Matthew,[17] which often considers the lowliest of Jewish society. These are the people Jesus is ministering to and beckoning into his kingdom. They are the ones who do not think they deserve to be there and who know that the religious elite do not want them. Jesus is speaking to the excluded, the weak and the overlooked.

Second, Jesus' words are spoken within the context of Roman occupation. All of the Jewish people are oppressed and feel controlled and manipulated by their overlords. Jesus is speaking to the oppressed.

Third, when we compare Matthew's Beatitudes with the blessings and woes in Luke,[18] we see that these words cannot simply be spiritualized in an unspecific way. Jesus is speaking to the poor. If they say anything to us about our spiritual lives (which I think they do), then that meaning must flow from the recognition of their specific context too; we cannot take the Beatitudes out of context. By understanding the context into which the Beatitudes are spoken, we can discover the core principles at their heart which can then be applied faithfully into our context.

These words begin to make more sense when we remember these three things. There is a special blessing in discovering you are welcomed and seen if you have spent your whole life thinking you are not wanted and that your community has excluded you. There is a special blessing in knowing that in your brokenness and pain, when you feel manipulated, controlled and oppressed, there is comfort and hope. And there is a blessing in knowing that your physical and social poverty are not the end of your story, that you are worth more than you think. It is only when we understand this that we can discover that:

Jesus proposes that it is possible to live in the confidence that we are under the favour of God. Of course such a privileged status is liable to make us happy from time to time, but while the feelings of happiness may come and go, the status of divine blessedness remains stable and secure. Our blessedness is assured not by personal circumstances nor by feelings, but by divine decree.[19]

Jesus, in sitting down to teach,[20] occupies the place of Moses once again. He positions himself before his audience as a lawgiver, whose words will have authority and significance in their lives. As he does so, he takes them on a journey from how *they* see themselves and their circumstances and into how *God* sees them. He is helping them to understand that the stories they have told themselves, and the stories they have been told by their culture and their religious leaders, are wrong. There is a better story. We find that better story in the second half of each of the Beatitudes:

Blessed are the poor in spirit, for theirs is the kingdom of heaven.
Blessed are those who mourn, for they will be comforted.
Blessed are the meek, for they will inherit the earth.
Blessed are those who hunger and thirst for righteousness, for they will be filled.
Blessed are the merciful, for they will receive mercy.
Blessed are the pure in heart, for they will see God.
Blessed are the peacemakers, for they will be called children of God.
Blessed are those who are persecuted for righteousness' sake, for theirs is the kingdom of heaven.
(Matthew 5.3–10)

So the first step in this upside-down set of principles that Jesus sets out is knowing that even when you are excluded, weak, overlooked, oppressed and poor, you matter to God. You are seen. You are known. You are welcome. The poor, or the poor in spirit, are not excluded; they are actually heirs of God's kingdom.

The fact that Jesus returns to this promise for those who are persecuted means that we can take everything in between as an inherent part of life in the kingdom of heaven. If you are an heir of the kingdom, then all of these promises are true for you.

Those who mourn are not trapped in their sadness and pain; there is comfort available for them and they will experience it.

Those who are meek, the people who feel disempowered and useless, will actually inherit the earth; they are not powerless after all.

The hungry will be fed, including those who hunger for meaning, significance and place in the family of God. They are not shut out; they are welcomed by the king and they will have their yearnings sated.

It turns out that mercy is not a fool's game. God sees those who show mercy and will show them mercy too.

To be innocent, honest and open, to hold no guile, to be compassionate, to have genuine motives and take people at their word and to seek to do the right thing before God and before other people (to be pure in heart) is not a waste of time because it carries the promise that you will see God. You will not be lost in the midst of everyone else. You will not miss out.

To be a peacemaker involves saying some hard things and making some hard choices. Peacekeeping and peacemaking are vastly different. The former avoids confrontation; the latter knows that it is unavoidable. Peacekeepers try to see everyone's point of view as equally valid, but peacemakers try to help people see each other, knowing that there may be wrongs that need to be righted and lies that need to be exposed. Jesus tells his listeners that when they seek to be peacemakers, they are so clearly demonstrating the heart of God that they will be called God's children. God's children tell the truth. God's children try to bring people together.

Christ reminds his followers that when they do the right thing, they will be persecuted, but he wants them to know that persecution does not mean they are excluded from the kingdom of heaven. Even if they are rejected, as long as they are doing the right thing and have pure motives, they are still the heirs to the kingdom.

The repeated blessing in verse 11 is an emphatic reminder to the listeners that they are not the first people to be marginalized or ridiculed or attacked for doing the right thing. In fact, Jesus makes it clear that when they are attacked, they should take it as proof that they are on the right track.

I wonder if there was a religious elite listening to all of this, or Roman soldiers. If there were, they must have scratched their heads in anger and disbelief as they heard Jesus paint such a vastly different picture of happiness and belonging from that which they were used to. The Beatitudes are an invitation into a new community, where the embrace of God is offered to the least, the last and the lost.

I think there is a parallel way of reading the Beatitudes that flows from the perspective I have outlined above. It does not replace it, and we cannot do away with the actual, rooted, transformative teaching of these eight promises, but it does extend the meaning and draw us into the rest of the Sermon on the Mount when taken alongside all that I have just said. These promises also offer a spiritual pathway to all who would follow Christ. They show eight steps that never end and will continually draw us into deeper fellowship with God and with one another. Let me explain.

First, we recognize our fragility and frailty and our brokenness – we are poor in spirit. We are honest with ourselves and with God. From such a posture we are able to see that there is hope because the kingdom of God is open to us. In fact, the kingdom of God is *only* open to those who are humble enough to enter it like a child, in humility and complete dependency on God.

This leads us to the second step – mourning. When we see our inadequacy and our failures, we are broken by them. We understand that we are trapped and that there is no way out. We need hope, and it is offered to us in the form of God's comfort. God will

125

not crush the broken. A bruised reed God will not break and a smouldering flax God will not snuff out.[21]

As we embrace the comfort of God, having acknowledged our brokenness and shame, we begin to realize that we are utterly dependent on God for grace and purpose. We rest in God's strength and receive God's succour and we grow in meekness, which is the focus of the third beatitude. As we enter this honest space of dependence, we begin to see what is possible in our lives, the ways in which we can make a difference, where we belong and what our lives can bring to the world, thus we inherit the earth as we move away from our rejection and shame and enter God's embrace and purposes for our lives.

Having tasted the mercy of God in the kingdom of heaven, we hunger and yearn for it. A desire to live in this space of honesty and freedom and hope consumes us, and God does not disappoint us. We are met by divine abundance in the hunger of our lives – God satisfies the hungry,[22] and all who taste and see will know the goodness of God.[23] Jesus will welcome all who come to him,[24] and will turn none of them away.[25]

The fifth step of this process is that, having tasted and experienced the mercy of God, we want others to experience it too. God's work in us continues through us as we share the mercy we have encountered. The more mercy we have experienced, the more we want to share.[26]

The next two steps are rooted in mercy. As we live in mercy, we long to stay close to God and for others to be close to God too. Our motives are filtered through the gossamer of grace and we are drawn into a journey of deeper holiness and intimacy as we seek to live in a way that brings us into alignment with God's purposes and plans. This in turn leads to a deeper sense of who God is and what God wants of us and of the world, and so we long for others to experience this peace with God, this new-found identity and freedom.

As God's children we seek to welcome new sisters and brothers into the family. But our living in this kingdom and for this King is not understood by the culture around us, meaning we are rejected and attacked for doing the right thing. This in turn exposes the continued work that needs to carry on in our hearts as our pride grows and our reactions display that there is much that still needs to change. And so we come to the beginning of the cycle again, as we face our inadequacy or hide it. Every time we face ourselves, we have a choice. We can spiral into God's grace or away from it.

Seeing both sides of the Beatitudes unlocks the rest of the Sermon on the Mount

It is only as we see both sides of these remarkable promises or blessings that we can make sense of the rest of the Sermon on the Mount. Both aspects would have been countercultural for the followers who were listening to Jesus. They needed to know that they were welcomed, and that their status was not dependent on their circumstances, but at the same time they knew, as all people know, that their lives were broken on the inside too. The rest of the teaching that Jesus brings to these people hinges on them understanding two seemingly contradictory ideas.

First, they are welcomed as they are and no one can exclude them. They are not judged by externals or by the culture and norms of the Jewish hierarchy, the Roman oppressors or the circumstances of their lives.

Second, the profound challenge laid at their feet requires them to interrogate their inner lives. They do not need a military messiah who will force out the Romans but a king who will bring them into a kingdom where they are able to be the people that their creator made them to be.

Salt and light: a reminder of vocation (Matt 5.13–16)

The next section of the Sermon on the Mount is both a promise and a challenge to Jesus' followers about how they view themselves and their purpose:

You are the salt of the earth; but if salt has lost its taste, how can its saltiness be restored? It is no longer good for anything, but is thrown out and trampled under foot.

You are the light of the world. A city built on a hill cannot be hidden. No one after lighting a lamp puts it under the bushel basket, but on the lampstand, and it gives light to all in the house. In the same way, let your light shine before others, so that they may see your good works and give glory to your Father in heaven.
(Matthew 5.13–16)

Applying to both their individual and their collective lives, Jesus encourages those to whom he speaks by reminding them that they have a purpose – they are salt and light and, as such, they are God's ambassadors to the world around them.[27] Both their individual choices and their witness as Israel is important and can have a formidable effect. They may be small, like salt and light, but they have a powerful significance if they live in the purposes and plans of the kingdom. Their attitudes and actions can shine into the darkness around them, stopping the rot of the culture and bringing the flavours of hope to the world. This is Eugene Peterson's paraphrasing of Matthew 5.13–16:

Let me tell you why you are here. You're here to be salt-seasoning that brings out the God-flavors of this earth. If you lose your saltiness, how will people taste godliness? You've lost your usefulness and will end up in the garbage.

Here's another way to put it: You're here to be light, bringing out the God-colors in the world. God is not a secret to be kept. We're going public with this, as public as a city on a hill. If I make you light-bearers, you don't think I'm going to hide you under a bucket, do you? I'm putting you on a light stand. Now that I've put you there on a hilltop, on a light

stand – shine! Keep open house; be generous with your lives.
By opening up to others, you'll prompt people to open up with
God, this generous Father in heaven.
(Matthew 5.13–16, THE MESSAGE)

But there is also a challenge in these words. As individuals and
as Israel, they must ensure that they remain salty, and that their
lights are lit and not hidden. Jesus reminds them that there are dire
consequences to ignoring the call to be distinct and faithful. Their
vocation is clear. They are to be the 'light of the world' and the 'salt
of the earth'. Their effectiveness is questionable.

It is this combination of promise and challenge that, in my
opinion, demands the double reading of the Beatitudes that I have
already set out. To suggest that Jesus' words in this chapter are
only about physical circumstances is to miss the way in which the
Beatitudes are connected to the rest of the Sermon. To suggest
that they are nothing other than spiritual aphorisms is to miss the
radical power that the first part of Matthew 5 holds to transform
lives. How are they to be distinct? What does it mean for them to
live in their God-given identity? The answer to those questions is
found in their ancient ways, customs and laws – in Torah. This is
precisely what Matthew tells us Jesus focuses on in the remainder
of this section of the Sermon on the Mount.

Torah and Prophets: the righteous and holy demands of God (Matt. 5.17–20)

Before he turns to the specifics of how they can know and strengthen
their distinct identity as kingdom people, Jesus must show them
that Torah still matters. This is precisely what he does in Matthew
5.17–20, which I have already explored in *Flipped*.[28] Jesus makes
clear to his followers that the demands of Torah and the promises
and declarations of the prophets still stand. They are not obstacles
to be overcome; they are signs that indicate what true life looks

like, and signposts that point to what liberation really means. By grounding the kingdom he is announcing in all that God has been saying and doing from the beginning, Jesus makes it clear that he has not come to do something novel, but instead that he has come to complete, to fulfil, to demonstrate and to solidify God's purposes in Israel and on the earth. In effect, Jesus is declaring that he is the cipher through which they can understand God, themselves and the world.

Having established the centrality of Torah in their lives and established before them that he is the living Torah, he turns their attention to how they are to live their lives clearly and faithfully, by visiting the teaching of Moses.

Liberated lives: a redefinition of freedom (Matt. 5.21–47)

Jesus now steers his listeners away from the folly of peer-to-peer comparison and relativism by confronting them with what a liberated life means. Positioning himself as one who is greater than Moses,[29] Jesus offers a bold and challenging revelation of the possibilities that holiness and faithfulness to God present to his followers. He does so by expanding on six key aspects of the Mosaic law: their understanding of anger;[30] adultery and sexual desire;[31] divorce;[32] promises;[33] retaliation;[34] and how to treat their enemies.[35]

In each of these examples, Jesus takes the teaching of Moses and presses further than his listeners have assumed or been taught it meant. Each time he says, 'You have heard it said . . . But I say to you . . .',[36] and in so doing reveals an antithesis between what they have read or been told in the law of Moses and what it means for them. He tells them that their inner lives and attitudes will shape their outer behaviour. He pushes past the way previous rabbis and teachers have interpreted Moses, using externals as their plumbline, and arrives at the point where he exposes the challenging reality that it is the inner life, the thoughts, intentions and attitudes of the heart, which is where the battle for liberation take place.

This is not a new idea to those listening; they would be familiar with the Proverbs of Solomon, which remind them that the way a person thinks in their heart determines who they are.[37] But by probing the meaning of Moses' teaching, Jesus is pushing them beyond external considerations and revealing that the heart is the central issue when it comes to holiness and abundant life.[38]

He is doing more than that, though – which is a marked departure from anything they have heard from a rabbi before. In probing Moses, he is going further than Moses has gone. This is nothing short of a moment of redefinition of their understanding of God's intention in the giving of Torah itself. I am not suggesting that Jesus is changing Torah, but he is certainly painting it with different colours and possibilities from anything that they have heard before, including what they have heard from Moses.

So murder, insults and derision all begin within us when we allow our attitudes to others to be soured or rooted in hatred and superiority. It is our hearts that must change. Similarly, adultery or lust does not happen with the act of physical sexual union; it begins when we think wrongly about someone, objectifying them and making them the subject of our secret fantasy or desire rather than seeing their dignity and worth. Jesus places a high value on the covenant of marriage, rooting it in the heart and not simply the externals of certification and legal documents, while at the same time challenging the way in which men have been given an unfair advantage over women in how a marriage is ended. He goes on to challenge the use of words, reminding his listeners that that their word should be their bond in every situation. He moves on to how they are to respond to aggression, calling them to a deeper moral place rather than simply lashing out, and he finally reminds them that they are to love those who oppose them, not just those who agree with them.

Jesus' teaching here is revolutionary. He is not only calling his listeners to a deeper and more intentional life, but he is also exposing the contradictions in their own hearts. He is demolishing any sense that to be holy or morally good is to behave in a certain way. Instead, he is reminding his listeners that those who follow him, kingdom people, are called to higher ethics and stronger morals in their inner lives. This is what will change their behaviour. It is only as they allow Torah to live in them that their outer lives, their behaviour, will change.

There are two other things going on here that are important to note.

Levelling up

First, Jesus is not only challenging the way in which the Jewish religious world has come to understand ethics and morals, but he is also challenging the way in which the oppressed Jews in Israel understand their relationship with their Roman oppressors and with each other. Jesus is telling them to remember their equal value and worth in relation to others. He is levelling up. The example of how they are to handle retaliation will be sufficient to demonstrate the point.

You have heard that it was said, 'An eye for an eye and a tooth for a tooth.' But I say to you, Do not resist an evildoer. But if anyone strikes you on the right cheek, turn the other also; and if anyone wants to sue you and take your coat, give your cloak as well; and if anyone forces you to go one mile, go also the second mile. Give to everyone who begs from you, and do not refuse anyone who wants to borrow from you.
(Matthew 5.38–42)[39]

We cannot overestimate the power of these insights around justice and ethics. Jesus is pushing beyond what they have been told Moses meant into new territory. He is directly reinterpreting the principles of justice and the boundaries of their social and civil obligations.[40] He uses five examples to demonstrate his deeper kingdom ethic: how to respond to being struck on the right cheek; what to do when someone demands your coat; how to respond to someone who asks you to go one mile; what to do when someone begs from you; and what to do when someone wants to borrow from you.

In Roman law, a Roman soldier could make certain demands of those over whom they ruled in occupied territories. For example, they could demand a coat, but not two coats; they could demand that someone carry their equipment for one mile, but not for two. In using both of these examples, Jesus is telling his listeners that they must learn how to engage in deeper acts of justice by going further than their oppressors can demand. In so doing, he is asserting that they are not less than the Romans who oppress them. They must learn to respond as equals. They cannot be forced to walk two miles or to offer their cloak as well as their coat, but by choosing to do so they move from a position of inferiority to a Roman soldier to a position of equality.

The same principle is true of Jesus' instruction around how to respond to a strike on the right cheek. To be slapped by someone in this way carried an inherent message of power. The person who hit you on the right cheek (the most important part of your body) would do so using the back of their left hand (the least important part of their body). The action carries with it an inherent message: that the person who slaps is superior to the person who is slapped. But to offer your left cheek (a less significant part of your body) to the person slapping demands that they use their right hand (a more significant part of their body) and sends the message to them that you are not their inferior; rather, you are their equal.

In the other two examples, of giving to someone who is begging and lending to someone who asks, Jesus reverses the message and is probably referring to life within the Jewish community rather than relationships with the Romans. When confronted with a beggar, his hearers are not to assume that they are superior to the beggar, but that they are equal. When confronted with a request involving borrowing, they are to move away from a place of control into a place of equality.

Grace takes us further: a new ethic

Second, Jesus is revealing that the kingdom he is establishing is one in which its people are able to go further than merely observing an external code. His work in their lives and his reign in the world do not mean that we can do what we want, or that there are no moral or ethical imperatives placed on the citizens of the kingdom. Quite the contrary – kingdom people can go further than those bound by an old, external reading of Torah. Jesus is drawing them into a deeper and higher moral code, not into a shallower and lower one.

Love (Matt. 5.43–47)

The sixth antithesis that Jesus confronts his audience with is the call to love. He tells them that they are not only to love the people whom it is easy to love – anyone can do that – but they are also to love their enemies and to pray for those who persecute them.

And so Matthew brings this section of Jesus' teaching full circle. Having warned them twice in the Beatitudes that they would be persecuted, Matthew tells us that Jesus instructs his listeners to love those who persecute them. Yet again, conventional wisdom is turned on its head.

These six antitheses do not just present Moses in a new way; they are going further into new revelation about what Torah and life in the kingdom actually mean. Jesus is painting a more demanding picture of life in the kingdom, not a less demanding one. His kingdom people are able to live differently because they see themselves differently, they see the world differently and they engage with others differently. They are released from trying to work out an external code and liberated into a life that flows from the ultimate call of Christ, which is proclaimed across all six of these antitheses.

Having told them that he has come to fulfil the law and the prophets, Jesus has painted a picture of what that means and used colours they have never seen before – the colours of a liberating love for God, for themselves and for others.

> When the Pharisees heard that he had silenced the Sadducees, they gathered together, and one of them, a lawyer, asked him a question to test him. 'Teacher, which commandment in the law is the greatest?' He said to him, '"You shall love the Lord your God with all your heart, and with all your soul, and with all your mind." This is the greatest and first commandment. And a second is like it: "You shall love your neighbour as yourself." On these two commandments hang all the law and the prophets.'
> (Matthew 22.34–40)

What all this means in a sentence (Matt. 5.48)

So Matthew brings us to the end of this rigorous self-examination. Having taught them who they are, why they are alive, what their purpose is and how they are to place themselves within the Great Story of God, he lays before them a demanding but liberating ethic which encompasses their personal and their community lives. He ends this inner journey of their ethics by calling them to perfection:

> Be perfect, therefore, as your heavenly Father is perfect.
> (Matthew 5.48)

His original listeners must have scratched their heads in bewilderment at such new teaching. It gave them the possibility of a completely different life and promised them a remarkable purpose, but it turned everything they had understood about themselves, or been taught, on its head.

It is helpful to see the Sermon as one great sweep of teaching with three movements. In the next movement in this great sweep, Jesus draws his listeners into the power, importance and motivation of their devotional lives by addressing the three key components of Jewish piety: giving to the poor;[41] prayer[42] and fasting;[43] and how they relate to their possessions[44] and their anxiety.[45] He tells them that the key to a life of contentment and peace is found not in hoarding things and accumulating wealth, but in generosity.[46] Once again, he upends their thinking. He links inner piety to their possessions, inner purpose to outer peace, and he tells them that they must choose what will dominate their lives. Yet he urges them to choose the kingdom because, in the end, it is putting the kingdom of God first that will bring peace and hope:

> But strive first for the kingdom of God and his righteousness, and all these things will be given to you as well.
> So do not worry about tomorrow, for tomorrow will bring worries of its own. Today's trouble is enough for today.
> (Matthew 6.33–34)

How we view others

And so we come to the last movement in Jesus' great sweeping Sermon on the Mount. In Matthew 7 he turns his attention to how his listeners view other people and, in particular, how they make judgements of others. Flipping their thinking yet again, he reminds them that they must use the same standards of judgement about themselves as they do about others, otherwise they are inviting more-severe judgement from God than they might want.[47] In case they think this means that they are never to make any judgements, however, he reminds them that they are entrusted with holy and powerful truths in all that he has just said and they are not to treat it lightly.[48] It is not that they are not to use judgement at all; it is that they are to use judgement properly.

At this point, I encourage you to pause and imagine that you are one of the people listening to Jesus. He has completely reframed your world. He has taught you about yourself, your worth and your purpose, but he has also reminded you of your duties and obligations. He has demanded a more ethical and moral life than anyone before him and he has called you to a more stringent control of your emotions and thought life than you have ever thought possible. He has exposed your brokenness and planted seeds of yearning around your emotions, your desires, your relationships, your words and your reactions to others and how you treat your enemies. He has called you to perfection. Then he turns his attention to your devotional life and how you handle possessions and wealth. He calls you to a higher level of giving, a deeper level of prayer and a more authentic level of fasting. He tells you to hold your possessions lightly and he calls you into a life of generosity and trust and away from a life of self-reliance and accumulation. He tells you to put the kingdom above everything else. Then he turns your mind to unfair judgements of others and he exposes your double standards, commanding you to make better judgements and to live a better life.

Surely, after hearing all of this, you would cry out to him and ask, 'How is this possible? Where do I get the strength, the wisdom and the power to live like this?' I think that is exactly the point, and Jesus gives his listeners the answer.

He tells them that if they ask God, they will be given the power to live like this. The key to this radically different living is not in them trying harder, but it is in their leaning into God and receiving the power and strength that God gives them to live as kingdom people in this radical, life-changing way. At this very point, Jesus tells them to ask, to seek and to knock – and to keep on doing so.[49] Indeed, in Luke's version of this instruction from Jesus, we are given even greater insight because Luke tells us that Jesus is specifically telling his followers to ask God for the power of the Holy Spirit to be at work in their lives.[50]

Right back at the beginning of Matthew's account of the Sermon on the Mount, we are told that Jesus says he has come to fulfil the law and the prophets. Now, as we approach the end of the Sermon, we are told what that means:

> In everything do to others as you would have them do to you; for this is the law and the prophets.
> (Matthew 7.12)

As I have already said, later in the gospel, Matthew points to loving God, loving others and loving ourselves as the fulfilment of the law and the prophets. I can only assume, therefore, that what we have in the Sermon on the Mount is an *a priori* explanation of what it means to love God, love others and love ourselves. This is what kingdom people are called to live in; it is what kingdom people are called to be.

Kingdom people do not treat others the way they treat us. Instead, we take the initiative by treating other people the way we *would want* them to treat us. This unique understanding of the Golden Rule means that we are no longer at the mercy of our circumstances or of what other people do to us. The Sermon on the Mount invites us to a life of liberation and freedom because it calls us into the divine plan of love for the world, before the world responds to us.

Finishing the Sermon, Jesus wants his followers to know that there are ways in which they can test the genuineness of their own faith and of the faith professions of others. First, there is the test of whether we do the popular thing or the right thing – will we go with the crowd or will we be willing to walk with the few?[51] Second, we are to remember that words and platitudes are not enough. If we are genuinely kingdom people, then there will be lasting fruit in our lives.[52] Third, we are to be careful to remember that it is not the claims that we make about ourselves that will determine whether or not we are kingdom people. Using the word 'Lord' does not necessarily mean that we believe Jesus is Lord; only living for him does that, and he will never be fooled by our false claims.[53]

The Sermon ends with Jesus telling his listeners that the genuineness of their faith will be shown when they face trials. It is what is left when the winds have come and the rains have fallen that is the evidence that matters. Are we building on sand or on rock?[54] In a little twist that modern hearers might miss, Jesus uses the images of building on sand and rock at a time when King Herod was known to be building himself a new house by the sea in Edessa. Herod, as King of Israel, is building foolishly, but Jesus, the true and lasting King of the kingdom, invites his kingdom people to build on the rock of who he is, what he says and what he has come to achieve.

Nothing could have been more revolutionary to his hearers. He beckoned them into a freedom that that they had never known, at a cost that they could not have counted.

He still does.

Let's pray

Giver of Life and Saviour of All,
We want to live for you.
Your Son's call to centre our inner world, outer world and relationships on your kingdom is so transforming and so demanding that we are left helpless and stuck without your power, but thank you that you do not ask us to live out of our own perspective.
Give us the ability to see the significance of the small, unnoticed work of your Spirit in our lives. Help us to see the power of the small and unnoticed acts of faithfulness in our lives that can bring glory and honour to your name and advance your kingdom.
Help us to walk in your ways, to listen for the heartbeat of your kingdom and to keep in step with your Spirit.
Fill us with your power, that we might live for you from the inside

of our worlds to the outside of our lives. May everything we do and everything we are be given to your kingdom.

Help us to notice what you notice.

Break our hearts with the things that break your heart.

Give us your responses to every situation that we face, and release your wisdom in our thinking.

Give us the gift of faith, we pray.

Give us the gifts of persistence and perseverance in our prayer, worship, devotion and service for you.

May our lives count for your kingdom.

Amen.

5

The promise of the kingdom

The world says, 'Become the boss.'
Jesus says, 'Become like a child.'

I first met Chris Simmons in 2010. His ministry changed my life.

Chris is the pastor of Cornerstone Baptist Church, Dallas. The church is in what was once the war zone of downtown Dallas. The area was blighted by drive-by shootings, littered with drug dens and awash with prostitution, violence and racial tension. In the 1960s and 1970s this once affluent part of Dallas began to run into more and more poverty as wealthier members of the community moved out of the city centre and toward more affluent and comfortable lifestyles in the ever-growing Metroplex. As the area fell deeper and deeper into recession and investment and business dried up, the housing stock in the area fell into disrepair and the community began to struggle. With no jobs, no income and no support, those who remained in the area (who were often the poorer, disenfranchised Black community) were drawn into violence, addiction and crime. The area became synonymous with the urban challenges of inner-city decline that would blight many industrialized nations.

When Chris arrived at Cornerstone Baptist Church, he was the latest in a long line of pastors who had come and then gone again very quickly. In one of his first conversations with a lady in the church, she told him that she gave him six months before he 'left, just like the rest'.

But Chris stayed.

And day by day, with hardly any income and no staff, God has used his ministry and his presence to see the area transformed.

Chris has given his whole life and ministry to serving one zip code in Dallas – the area around his church. His story is one of dogged commitment and pouring his life into the community. He has persuaded wealthier churches to send teams to help in the area around the church building. His only requirement is that when they partner with his church, they use the name of Cornerstone Baptist Church and make it clear that they are not coming as White saviours to a Black community. He stood up to racial violence before anyone else in Dallas. He knew Black Lives Matter before the slogan was used.

House by house, life by life, he has seen God do a work of transformation in his community. Former drug dens became drop-ins. A brothel became a halfway house for prisoners. A liquor store became a food bank. A rundown crack house became a community facility for people starting out in life who needed a safe, clean and hopeful place to stay. Chris persuaded some people to buy building lots (which were cheap because no one wanted them) and build new family homes for themselves, or for someone else to occupy.

Take a look at the church's website[1] and you will see that it runs a community kitchen, a clothing exchange, a shower and cleaning facility, a laundromat, a women's refuge, a drug rehabilitation centre, a community market, a house-building programme, a dental clinic, a daily school and pre-school, a medical centre, a child-minding service, a children's enrichment programme, a recycling centre, a bicycle refurbishment and distribution service, a food bank, an academy, a mentoring and prisoner rehabilitation programme, a jobs club, a young mothers and babies-at-risk service and a debt advice centre. All this runs alongside a fully functioning set of Sunday services, prayer gatherings and discipleship programme.

What is remarkable about all of this is that the average offerings at the church are low – between $5 and $10 a week per family. Chris and his family live simple, unpretentious lives. The church draws in support from larger, wealthier churches and welcomes teams from anywhere that will help, but its understanding of ministry, mission and discipleship is rooted in whole-life transformation. Cornerstone is not made up of wealthy, powerful, influential people in any terms that would be recognized by American or European society or politicians. The church is made up of those whose lives were, or are, broken and fragile. Yet it is one of the most beautiful communities of people who are seeking to follow Jesus that I have ever seen. It is a living embodiment of the truth that 'the last will be first and the first will be last'.[2] Day in and day out, this remarkable church is demonstrating the principles of community, kindness, compassion and human dignity that are embedded in the biblical call to transformation.

The church has had such an impact on the community that the city of Dallas has renamed the area in which it sits. Once upon a time the district was known for its drive-by shootings, its high level of drugs-related deaths and its violence. It is now called 'Cornerstone District' and is a flagship example of what happens when one Christian invests his or her life in an area and one church commits itself to living out the principles of the flipped kingdom – where God's view of people and places shapes everything else. The church, and the district, are regularly featured in press stories.[3]

I once asked Chris for advice. I wanted to know what the secret of this remarkable ministry was. He smiled, looked at me with loving eyes and said, 'Malcolm, remember that there is only one hero in this church, and his name ain't Chris.' Chris Simmons understands that there is only room for one central figure in the church – and his name is Jesus. Chris has eschewed writing articles or books or peddling his story around the world. He rejects suggestions that the story of Cornerstone is a story of renewal or revival. He doesn't speak at lots of conferences. He doesn't appear on the front of magazines. When the press tells the story of the community, it tells the story of the whole church and the whole community – it doesn't tell Chris's story. That is because Chris sees the story of Cornerstone as the simple story of what all churches should be like and what all Christian leaders are called to be. For him, Cornerstone is just the church being the church. His is a story of 'power . . . made perfect in weakness'.[4] Chris does not see himself as the centre of Cornerstone Baptist Church – that position is already taken.

When I think of Chris Simmons and Cornerstone Baptist Church, Dallas, Texas, they are emblematic of hundreds of churches that I have visited, served or been connected to over the years. These are local churches going about the work of the kingdom of God without shouting about it. From Willowfield Church in Belfast to St Mungo's in Edinburgh, from St Mark's in Dublin to City Church Cardiff in Wales, from Vibe in Armagh to Fishponds Baptist Church in Bristol, from Mortimer West End Chapel to BH1 Elim in Bournemouth, there are thousands of local churches across the UK and tens of thousands more across the rest of the world where the daily call to serve the community, welcome the stranger and love the lost is having a remarkable effect.

God's kingdom is not primarily advanced through exciting conferences and big events (although they have their place), and megachurches are not the norm. It isn't the stories from churches that are plastered across Instagram, Facebook and Twitter that will see the world transformed (I thank God for all these good news stories – I just don't think they are the whole story!). The work of God's kingdom has always been advanced most powerfully by the unnoticed, unseen and uncelebrated ministries of ordinary women and men and by small churches with hardly any money and tiny staff teams.

God flips the idea of success so that it includes perseverance, small acts of kindness, tiny wins and baby steps forward. God doesn't only celebrate the big and the flashy; God endorses the small and the unnoticed. God is more interested in people than in programmes and more committed to whole-life discipleship and lives of faithful flourishing than to tokenistic conversions and completed decision cards. Kingdom people have a simple and straightforward trust that their small acts of kindness, compassion and faithfulness are seeds of hope planted in the soil of the earth and will change the world by God's grace. We aren't in charge; God is. We are simply God's children, living God's way – and that changes everything. God is always in charge.

Michael Green highlights four aspects of what 'the kingdom of heaven' means:

1 It points to the ultimate sovereignty of God in the world.
2 It stakes a claim on the lives of those who claim to follow Christ.
3 It describes the realm in which this reign is acknowledged (we enter it like a little child, and we receive the kingdom by surrendering to its King and being obedient to its principles and his rule – Matthew 18.1–9; 19.14).
4 It points to a future reality where all of God's rule and reign will be shown fully on the earth as it is in heaven.[5]

As Green's fourth point shows, Matthew presents the kingdom of heaven as not only here, but also a future promise and soon-to-be reality,[6] to which we will return. This future aspect of the kingdom lingers mysteriously across the scroll of his gospel like a scented promise of restoration and renewal, but it also whispers a warning to those who think that they should be given places of honour, prestige and power.

> Truly I tell you, there are some standing here who will not taste death before they see the Son of Man coming in his kingdom.
> (Matthew 16.28)

> And he said to her, 'What do you want?' She said to him, 'Declare that these two sons of mine will sit, one at your right

hand and one at your left, in your kingdom.' But Jesus answered, 'You do not know what you are asking. Are you able to drink the cup that I am about to drink?' They said to him, 'We are able.' He said to them, 'You will indeed drink my cup, but to sit at my right hand and at my left, this is not mine to grant, but it is for those for whom it has been prepared by my Father.' (Matthew 20.21–23)

It is important to be clear about something here, though. Far too much time is spent talking about a future kingdom that will be set up by Jesus that is not connected to his current rule and reign now. The future aspect of the kingdom is not the point at which it is established – that has already happened. There will be a consummation when Christ returns, but the kingdom of God is present now and Jesus is its King. To suggest otherwise is to fly in the face of the New Testament's evidence and to create a pie-in-the-sky-when-you-die kind of spirituality that denudes the call to Christian discipleship of its dynamic kingdom edge. The kingdom has come in Christ, and it remains through his regency and is evidenced in his people.

Jesus' kingdom has not been deferred until his return or until after he is able to 'clean house' at the final judgment. He will return, and there will be a settling of accounts, we can be sure of this. But until then, he is not biding his time, having been limited to changing a few minds here and there, saving individual souls at various religious services, making a few mystical appearances now and again, until some unknown period in the future when he can get his original intentions back on track . . . Jesus' rule began when he said it did, at the proclamation of his 'Great Commission'.[7]

Returning to our roots

The book of Acts shows us a community, or perhaps even communities, that were living out these powerful, radical, upside-down principles in their day-to-day lives. Theirs was a life of radical openness to the Holy Spirit, radical community, radical generosity and radical mission. Acts offers us little cameos of this upside-down living and reminds us of the power of this witness.

> All who believed were together and had all things in common; they would sell their possessions and goods and distribute the proceeds to all, as any had need. Day by day, as they spent much time together in the temple, they broke bread at home and ate their food with glad and generous hearts, praising God and having the goodwill of all the people. And day by day the Lord added to their number those who were being saved.
> (Acts 2.44–47)

> Now the whole group of those who believed were of one heart and soul, and no one claimed private ownership of any possessions, but everything they owned was held in common. With great power the apostles gave their testimony to the resurrection of the Lord Jesus, and great grace was upon them all. There was not a needy person among them, for as many as owned lands or houses sold them and brought the proceed of what was sold. They laid it at the apostles' feet, and it was distributed to each as any had need.
> (Acts 4.32–35)

> As they left the council, they rejoiced that they were considered worthy to suffer dishonour for the sake of the name. And every day in the temple and at home they did not cease to teach and proclaim Jesus as the Messiah.
> (Acts 5.41–42)

The word of God continued to spread; the number of the disciples increased greatly in Jerusalem, and a great many of the priests became obedient to the faith.
(Acts 6.7)

Meanwhile the church throughout Judea, Galilee, and Samaria had peace and was built up. Living in the fear of the Lord and in the comfort of the Holy Spirit, it increased in numbers.
(Acts 9.31)

And immediately, because he had not given the glory to God, an angel of the Lord struck him down, and he was eaten by worms and died.
   But the word of God continued to advance and gain adherents.
(Acts 12.23–24)

So the churches were strengthened in the faith and increased in numbers daily.
(Acts 16.5)

So the word of God grew mightily and prevailed.
(Acts 19.20)

He [Paul] lived there for two whole years at his own expense and welcomed all who came to him, proclaiming the kingdom of God and teaching about the Lord Jesus Christ with all boldness and without hindrance.
(Acts 28.30–31)

This countercultural community blazed a trail of hope and faith across the known world. Seeking to live out the call and the commands of their Saviour, they were radically brave in their message and its delivery; they were radically inclusive in who could join them while also being radically transformative in their call to discipleship; they were radically committed to one another in prayer, generosity and lifestyle; they were radically free in their refusal to call anyone except Jesus their Lord; and they were radically adventurous in their journeys of faith. They challenged the norms and expected priorities of the cities they visited and the cultures they were immersed in – from the idolatry of Ephesus to the political rigidity of Rome, from the sexual licentiousness of Corinth and Colossae to the economic superiority and manipulation of Philippi and Laodicea. They stood before proconsuls, governors, high priests and emperors and remained true to the call of Christ. Everyone they engaged with noticed how different they were. In Thessalonica, their demeanour and their message caused a riot. They were dragged into court where a charge was laid against them:

These people who have been turning the world upside down
have come here also.
(Acts 17.6)

You could disagree with this early band of Jesus' followers. You could resent them, endorse them, reject them, love them or hate them, but you could not ignore them.

Christopher Hill, the English historian, borrowed a phrase from Acts 17.6 when he wrote a history of some of the radical ideas of the puritans and church movements of the English Revolution. He entitled his book *The World Turned Upside Down: Radical Ideas During the English Revolution*.[8] He sees the radical ideas of the Reformation church as carrying the potential to change society in England:

There had been moments when it seemed as though from the
ferment of radical ideas a culture might emerge which might

be different both from the traditional aristocratic culture and from the bourgeois culture of the protestant ethic which replaced it. We can discern shadows of what this counter-culture might have been like. Rejecting private property for communism, religion for rationalistic and materialistic pantheism, the mechanical philosophy for dialectical science, asceticism for unashamed enjoyment of the good things of the flesh, it might have achieved unity through a federation of communities, each based on the fullest respect for the individual. Its ideal would have been economic self-sufficiency, not world trade or world domination. The economic significant consequence of the Puritan emphasis on sin was the compulsion on labour, to save, to accumulate, which contributed so much to making the Industrial Revolution possible in England. Ranters simply rejected this; Quakers ultimately came to accept it. Only Winstanley put forward an alternative . . . It came nearest to realisation in the Digger communities, which might have given the counter-culture some economic base.[9]

Whether you agree with Hill's observation of this period or history or not is irrelevant. I read his book on this period just a few months after I became a Christian. I was young, passionate and longing to see God use me and touch the church. I remember asking myself then if the people of Northern Ireland saw the church as a community that was turning the world upside down. Is that how people in Europe, the United States of America and the United Kingdom now see us? Do we still have this raw, society-transforming, life-changing reputation? I have no doubt that some local churches could be described as this. But can this be said of the church in general? If not, then why not? Is it even something that we long for? What if it is what the world needs us to be? What if the only church that has anything to say to our culture is a church that is so radically different from the world around us that we can be described as turning the world upside down?

The author and cultural commentator, Mark Sayers, believes that God is raising up a new, radical mindset and cry in Christians:

Around the word, within the church and outside of it, there is a grouping of people that remain largely unnamed. They are unnamed, ignored by the chattering classes because they quietly are getting on with the job. They are founding not-for-profits, planting churches, creating new ministries, starting new businesses, advocating for causes. Our culture of deconstruction that has come to dominate the church no longer helps them. It hinders them. They are the rebuilders, partners with God in the rebuilding of His creational order.[10]

Back in 2013, I wrote a book called *Risk Takers*,[11] exploring the call of God upon us as individuals to lead a life of uninhibited worship, devotion and service. In some ways, what I am now writing is an invitation to the *whole* church to return to a call to be radically different from the world and radically faithful to Jesus.

It pains me to admit that I think much of the church of our generation has lost its radical, kingdom edge. We have, too often, allowed ourselves to be drawn into the traps that Jesus so clearly avoided. When satan tempted Jesus,[12] he offered him the triple lure of relevance, stardom and power. Jesus rejected them all – but I fear that much of the modern church has fallen foul of this ancient seduction. We have allowed ourselves to set relevance as more important than authenticity, stardom as more important than faithfulness, and power as more important than influence. As a result, we have gained relevance, stardom and power but we have lost authenticity, faithfulness and influence. To borrow from the life of Esau, we have sold our birthright for a bowl of stew.[13]

Called to be a community of Jesus' followers whose lives challenge the norms of our society as we bring out the 'God-colors (*sic*) in the world',[14] we have too often settled for being a pale imitation of our culture, reflecting our society's priorities rather than shining a light on them. We have become mirrors of the world around us rather than mirrors of God's value and hope.

Commenting in 1984 specifically on the slide of the evangelical church in the United States of America into what he described as an accommodation of the spirit of the age, Francis Schaeffer wrote:

> This accommodation has been costly, first in destroying the power of the Scriptures to confront the spirit of our age; second in allowing the further slide of our culture. Thus we must say with tears that it is the evangelical accommodation to the world spirit around us, to the wisdom of this age, which removes the evangelical church from standing against further breakdown in our culture. It is my firm belief that when we stand before Jesus Christ, we will find that it has been the weakness and accommodation of the evangelical group in the issues of the day that has been largely responsible for the loss of the Christian ethos which has taken place in the area of culture in our own country over the last forty to sixty years.[15]

But all is not lost. As Mark Sayers notes above, there are many who are shifting. Disillusioned with what they consider consumerism, entertainment and superficiality, many Christians are turning away from small theologies of services and sermons to a bigger picture of the church as an agent of the kingdom of God. Over the last few years, no doubt budged by the pandemic and the insecurity of our world, I have heard leaders speak of a yearning for more, or a hunger to pursue God's purposes in a deeper, more meaningful way. Disillusioned with what they have experienced in church, these women and men are looking for something better. They recognize that God's concern is not merely to satisfy the misplaced dreams and goals of women and men, but rather to 'turn people away from their self-centredness and obsession with temporal, material concerns and to draw them into a relationship with himself so they are his instruments for accomplishing his purposes'.[16]

In essence, followers of Christ are returning to their roots – to the call of Christ to follow him in life and to follow him in death. This call is captured beautifully in the lyrics of a song, 'Hear the Call of the Kingdom', written by Stuart Townend and Keith and Kristyn Getty in 2006. The song invites us to lift our eyes to heaven and to the kingdom of God, and let King Jesus shape our thinking, our imaginations and our lives.

Just imagine

There is much at stake as we embark on this journey together. It could change our lives, but it could also change the world. Our cultures are crying out for a visible, tangible expression of hope. Again and again I speak to people who want to belong to something. The greatest and fullest days of God's kingdom could lie ahead of us.

It is possible that the words spoken by the prophet Haggai are more relevant now than they have ever been. Prophesying in the last quarter of 520 BC, he called the people of God to re-engage in the task of building the temple. They had been back in Jerusalem for around 17 years, having been released from their captivity by God through the decisions of the Medo-Persian emperor Cyrus.

Having returned to Jerusalem to rebuild the temple that had been destroyed by the Babylonians in 586 BC, they had faltered. Maybe they were discouraged? Maybe they were weary? Maybe they had forgotten why they went back to Jerusalem in the first place? Maybe the opposition they faced was overwhelming? Maybe they had just settled? It is probably the case that all these reasons, and many more, had caused their work to stop. Haggai was raised by God to call them back to the work.

In a short series of prophetic messages delivered by Haggai between August and December 520 BC, God raised the eyes of the Hebrew people again and reminded them that God wanted them to finish the work. Haggai called them forward into a new season by saying:

> Who is left among you that saw this house in its former glory? How does it look to you now? . . . Yet now take courage . . . says the LORD; take courage . . . take courage, all you people of the land, says the LORD; work, for I am with you, says the LORD of hosts, according to the promise that I made you when you came out of Egypt. My spirit abides among you; do not fear . . . Once again, in a little while, I will shake the heavens and the earth and the sea and the dry land; and I will shake all the nations, so that the treasure of all nations shall come, and I will fill this house with splendour, says the LORD of hosts. The silver is mine, and the gold is mine, says the LORD of hosts. The latter splendour of this house shall be greater than the former, says the LORD of hosts; and in this place I will give prosperity, says the LORD of hosts.
> (Haggai 2.3–9)

These words, spoken about God's people, Israel, and referring to the rebuilding of the temple in Jerusalem, called a discouraged and weary people back into action for their God. I am convinced that a fresh vision of the upside-down kingdom will do the same for us. We can be flipped out of weariness and into energy, out of apathy and into anticipation, out of fear and into faith, out of defeat and into victory. What lies ahead is a brighter, clearer and stronger vision of what we do when we worship, pray, give, preach, serve and live intentionally in the world for Christ.

The church is an embassy for the kingdom. We are called to show the values and the vision of God's reign and rule in the world. Nothing could be more daunting, but nothing could be more exciting. I invite you into the journey with me and pray that God will meet us as we walk.

With Tom Wright, I invite you into a:

> . . . new reality of a story so explosive . . . that the church in many generations has found it too much to take and so has watered it down, cut it up into little pieces, turned it into small-scale lessons rather than allowing its full impact to be felt. Part of the tragedy of the modern church . . . is that the 'orthodox' have preferred creed to Kingdom, and the 'unorthodox' have tried to get a Kingdom without a creed. It's time to put back together what should never have been separated. In Jesus, the living God has become king of the whole world. These books [the gospels] not only tell the story of how that happened. They are the central means by which those who read and pray them can help to make that Kingdom a reality in tomorrow's world. We have misunderstood the gospels for too long. It's time, in the power and joy of the spirit, to get back on track.[17]

Let's pray

Our God and our King – let your kingdom come!
Thank you for your kingdom in all of its beauty and power – let your kingdom come!
Thank you for the call to be your subjects. Help us to celebrate and live under your headship and rule, King Jesus – let your kingdom come!
Help us to lean into and rely on your power, Holy Spirit – let your kingdom come!
Help us, in all that we are and in all that we do, to live for your glory, Father – let your kingdom come!

May we show people our King – let your kingdom come!
May we live as your people – let your kingdom come!
May we give ourselves to your purpose – let your kingdom come!
May we look at the world with your perspective – let your kingdom come!
May we hold on to your vision – let your kingdom come!
Your Son is our King. He is life to us, and without him we can do nothing. So give us the faith to believe that you have not finished with us and that he is still at work in us. We welcome the prodding and prompting of your Holy Spirit and we pray that you would give us sanctified and redeemed imaginations – let your kingdom come!
Help us to dream again for you – let your kingdom come!
Help us to go again for You – let your kingdom come!
Help us to step into the unknown again for you – let your kingdom come!
Where we are jaded, shake away our cynicism – let your kingdom come!
Where we are hurt, bring healing – let your kingdom come!
Where we are frightened, release faith – let your kingdom come!
Where we are weary, bring fresh energy – let your kingdom come!
Where we are confused, bring wisdom – let your kingdom come!
Where we are broken, use our fragility to shine your grace into the world – let your kingdom come!
In our lives, in our homes, in our streets, in our communities, in our churches, in our nations and in our world, let your kingdom come!
Our Father,
Who art in heaven,
Hallowed be thy name!
Thy kingdom come!
Thy will be done,
On earth as it is in heaven.
Give us this day our daily bread,

And forgive us our trespasses,
As we forgive those who trespass against us.
And lead us not into temptation,
But deliver us from evil.
For thine is the kingdom, the power and glory,
For ever and ever,
Amen.

Notes

An invitation: Learning to live again

1 Gutiérrez, G., translated by O'Connell, M. J. (1991), *The God of Life* (Maryknoll, New York: Orbis Books), p. 89.
2 Gutiérrez, G., translated by O'Connell, M. J. (1984), *We Drink from Our Own Wells: The Spiritual Journey of a People* (Maryknoll, New York: Orbis Books), p. 38. Heli, Tibur (2016), 'Encountering God in the Face of the Poor According to Gustavo Gutierrez'. 南山神学, 39: 159–79, p. 159.
3 Gutiérrez, G., translated by Inda, C. and Eagleson, J. (1973), *A Theology of Liberation: History, Politics, and Salvation* (Maryknoll, New York: Orbis Books), p. 115.
4 Gutiérrez, *A Theology of Liberation*, p. 116.
5 Gutiérrez, *A Theology of Liberation*, p. 118.
6 Habakkuk 2.14.
7 Genesis 1.26–28.
8 Psalm 139.14.
9 Luke 14.21.
10 Mark 5.
11 John 4.
12 Luke 10.38–42.
13 Luke 18.35–43.
14 1 Samuel 16.7.
15 Genesis 4.
16 Matthew 8.1–4.
17 Mark 2.1–12.
18 Leviticus 19.34.
19 Psalm, 118.22; Matthew 21.42; 1 Peter 2.7.
20 1 Peter 2.8.
21 2 Samuel 9.

22 For example, see 'Kingdom People', Diocese of Worcester (2022),
    <www.cofe-worcester.org.uk/Kingdom-people> (accessed 3
    November 2022); 'What We Do', Cornerstone Baptist Church (2022),
    <www.cornerstonedallas.org/what-we-do> (accessed 3 November
    2022); Wright, D. (2022), 'Christians Are Called to Be a Kingdom
    People', Vineyard Churches, <www.vineyardchurches.
    org.uk/resources/christians-are-called-to-be-a-Kingdom-people>
    (accessed 3 November 2022). See also Jenkins, D. (2013), *Kingdom
    People Living by Kingdom Principles: A Holistic Approach to the
    Call of Missions* (Bloomington: Westbow Press); Faith and Order
    Commission (2020), *Kingdom Calling: The Vocation, Ministry and
    Discipleship of the Whole People of God* (London: Church House
    Publishing); Bown, D. (2019), *Kingdom People: How We Created
    Spiritual and Social Renewal in a Marginalised Society* (Darlington:
    McKnight & Bishop Inspire).
23 For an excellent bibliography of twentieth-century scholarship
    and research on the kingdom of God, see Chrupcała, L. (2022),
    'The Kingdom of God: A Bibliography of 20th Century Research.
    Update', *Academia.edu*, <www.academia.edu/41346521/The
    _Kingdom_of_God_A_Bibliography_of_20th_Century_Research.
    _Update> (accessed 3 November 2022).

Introduction: The 'flipped' foundations

1 Green, M. (2000), *The Message of Matthew* (Nottingham: Inter-
   Varsity Press), p. 43.
2 For an excellent summary of the kingdom in the teaching of Jesus,
   see Ladd, G. E. (1966), *Jesus and the Kingdom: Scriptural Studies in
   the Kingdom of God* (London: SPCK).
3 Ladd, *Jesus and the Kingdom*, pp. 43–7.
4 Matthew 3.2; 4.8, 17, 23; 5.3, 10, 19, 20; 6.10, 33; 7.21; 8.10–12; 9.35;
   10.7–8; 11.11–12; 12.28; 13.11, 14, 24, 31, 33, 38, 41, 43, 44, 45, 47, 52;
   16.19; 18.1, 3, 4; 19.12, 14, 23, 24; 20.1; 21.31, 43; 22.2; 25.1, 31, 34, 40;
   26.29; 27.11, 29, 37, 42.
5 Matthew 6.9.
6 Matthew 18.23–35.

7   Matthew 26.26.

8   Matthew 6.10.

9   See Matthew 1.18.

10 See Matthew 1.23 and Isaiah 7.14; Matthew 2.5–6 and Micah. 5.2–3;
    Matthew 2.15 and Hosea 11.1; Matthew 2.18 and Jeremiah 31.15,
    Genesis 42.13, 26 and Lamentations 5.7; Matthew 2.23 and the
    implication that the Messiah, like the Nazarenes, would be despised
    and eschewed – a sentiment found in passages such as Psalm 22.6,
    Isaiah 49.7; 53.3 and Daniel 9.16. See also the way in which Nazareth
    was viewed at the time – John 1.46; 7.41, 52. Or perhaps Matthew
    2.23 is an example of Matthew using a wordplay with Isaiah 11.1,
    because the word for 'Nazareth' sounds like the word for 'branch' in
    Hebrew – a designation of the Messiah. Note that identification of
    Jesus as a Nazarene has no connection with the nazirites of the Old
    Testament – see Numbers 6.2 and Judges 13.5 for more information.

11 Matthew 2.11.

12 Matthew 1.20–24.

13 Matthew 2.12, 13, 19 and perhaps 22, although no angel is specifically
    mentioned there.

14 Matthew 8 and 9.

15 Matthew 17.1–13.

16 Matthew 12.1–14.

17 Matthew 21.23–27

18 Matthew 12.22–32

19 Matthew 25.31.

20 Matthew 25.31–46.

21 Matthew 25.34, 46.

22 Matthew 16.24–26.

23 Matthew 10.23; 24.1–2.

24 Matthew 26.63–64.

25 Matthew 26.64.

26 Green, *The Message of Matthew*, p. 45. Reflect also on Acts 8.12; 19.8;
    20.25; 28.23 and 28.31, where the kingdom is proclaimed as Christ is
    proclaimed.

27 Matthew presents ideas of repentance eight specific times in his

gospel. He mentions it three times in reference to the ministry of John the Baptist in Matthew 3 – in verses 2, 8 and 11. He connects it to Jesus directly in Matthew 4.17; 11.20, 21 and 12.41. His last use of the term is in Matthew 27.3 in connection to Judas. The idea must also play heavily in his mind when he portrays Jesus as telling us that we must be humble and like little children if we are to enter the kingdom – see Matthew 18.3, 6.

28 Green, *The Message of Matthew*, p. 45.

29 Matthew 5—7.

30 Gladden, W. (1894), *The Church and the Kingdom* (New York: Fleming H. Revell), p. 5.

31 Matthew 16.18 and 18.17. Although the NRSVA uses the word 'church' in Matthew 18.15 and 21, this is a choice of translation to represent inclusivity in the community of faith – the original text refers to a 'brother' in both instances. My own view is that the use of the word 'church' here is misplaced by the translators and that a better phrase to adopt as inclusive would be 'a person in the family of faith'.

32 Matthew 3.2; 4.8, 17, 23; 5.3, 10, 19, 20; 6.10, 33; 7.21; 8.11, 12; 9.35; 10.7; 11.11, 12; 12.25, 26, 28; 13.11, 19, 24, 31, 33, 38, 41, 43, 44, 45, 47, 52; 16.19, 28; 18.1, 3, 4, 23; 19.12, 14, 23, 24; 20.1, 21; 21.31, 43; 22.2; 23.13; 24.7, 14; 25.1, 34; 26.29. Mark records the use of the word 18 times – Mark 1.15; 3.24; 4.11, 26, 30; 6.23; 9.1, 47; 10.14, 15, 23, 24, 25; 11.10; 12.34; 13.8; 14.25; 15.43; Luke 42 times – Luke 1.33; 4.5, 43; 6.20; 7.28; 8.1, 10; 9.2, 11, 27, 60, 62; 10.9, 11; 11.2, 17, 18, 20; 12.31, 32; 13.18, 20, 28, 29; 14.15; 16.16; 17.20, 21; 18.16, 17, 24, 25, 29; 19.11; 21.10, 31; 22.16, 18, 29; 23.42, 51 and John three times – John 3.3, 5; 18.36.

33 Fairbairn, A. M. (1893), *The Place of Christ in Modern Theology*, 2nd edn (London: Hodder & Stoughton), p. 515.

34 Matthew 16.18 – one of the two places cited above where Christ is quoted as using the word *ekklesia* which we translate as 'church'.

35 Matthew 4.23 and Matthew 9.35, for example. See also Mark 1.14 and Luke 8.1.

36 Matthew 13.3, 19, 23.

37 Matthew 14.19; 18.4 and 19.12.

38 Matthew 12.28 (cf. 26). See also Luke 11.20 (cf. 17, 18).

39 I do not capitalize the word 'satan', believing it not to be a name but a description of the devil.

40 Matthew 5.3; 12.28. See also Luke 17.21 and Mark 10.14.

41 Matthew 21.31.

42 Matthew 11.11. See also Luke 7.28.

43 Fairbairn, *The Place of Christ in Modern Theology*, p. 517.

44 Green, *The Message of Matthew*, p. 46.

45 Matthew 13.1–9.

46 Matthew 7.15–23; 24.11.

47 Matthew 13.21; 24.9–10.

48 Matthew 13.12.

49 Green, *The Message of Matthew*, pp. 46–7.

50 Matthew 6.13.

51 Matthew 12.22–32.

52 Matthew 13.36–43, quoting vv. 37–39.

53 Matthew 4.1–11.

54 Matthew 12.28–29.

55 Matthew 16.21–23, particularly v. 23.

56 Matthew 11.16–19.

57 Matthew 16.1–4 and the use of the term 'evil' in v. 4.

58 Ephesians 6.10ff.

59 2 Corinthians 11.14.

60 Lewis makes mention of this idea in several guises. He is an occultic scientist in Lewis's work, *That Hideous Strength*, and he is Uncle Andrew, who brings sin to Narnia, in *The Magician's Nephew*. Lewis, C. S. (2012), *That Hideous Strength* (New York: Harper One). Lewis, C. S. (2009), *The Magician's Nephew (The Chronicles of Narnia, Book 1)* (London: HarperCollins). For more on this theme, see Veith, G. E. (2005), *Soul of the Lion, the Witch, and the Wardrobe* (Colorado Springs: Victor), particularly pp. 123–48 and pp. 163–80.

61 Lewis, C. S. (1982), *The Screwtape Letters* (New York: Bantam Books), p. 19ff.

62 Sproul, R. C. (2017), *The R. C. Sproul Collection, Volume 2* (Carol

Stream: Tyndale House Publishers, Inc.). See particularly chapter 48, entitled 'Satan'.

1 King of the kingdom

1 Tutu, D. (1995), *An African Prayer Book* (New York: Doubleday), p. 80.

2 Linney, G. (2022), 'Thinking Anew – Love Is Stronger Than Hate', *Irish Times*, <www.irishtimes.com/news/social-affairs /religion-and-beliefs/thinking-anew-love-is-stronger-than-hate 1.4778712#:~:text=At%20the%20core%20of%20who,through%20 Him%20who%20loves%20us> (accessed 7 November 2022).

3 Huddleston, T. (1956), *Naught for Your Comfort* (London: Collins).

4 Wright, T. (2012), *How God Became King: Getting to the Heart of the Gospels* (London: SPCK), p. x.

5 Tutu, D., Mutloatse, M. and Webster, J. (1984), *Hope and Suffering* (Glasgow: Collins Fount), pp. 79–80.

6 See Lierman, J. (2004), *The New Testament Moses: Christian Perceptions of Moses and Israel in the Setting of Jewish Religion* (Tübingen: Mohr Siebeck). Lierman's doctoral thesis is a powerful and insightful analysis of the importance of Moses to the Jewish faith at the time of Jesus' earthly ministry, a period also known as Second Temple Judaism.

7 Porter, J. R. (1963), *Moses and Monarchy: A Study in the Biblical Tradition of Moses* (Oxford: Blackwell). Porter sets out a convincing picture of the kingly understanding of Moses set out in the Hebrew Bible, particularly in the Pentateuch and the Former Prophets.

8 Lierman, *The New Testament Moses*, p. 79f.

9 Meeks, Wayne A., edited by Van Unnik, W. C. (1967), *The Prophet-King: Moses Traditions and the Johannine Christology*. Supplements to Novum Testamentum (Leiden: E. J. Brill). See p. 188 for the significance of the sceptre.

10 Lierman, *The New Testament Moses*, pp. 85ff.

11 For a remarkable exploration of the way in which Eusebius compares Jesus to Moses, see Bruns, J. E. (1977), 'The "Agreement of Moses and Jesus" in the "Demonstratio Evangelica" of Eusebius', *Vigiliae*

Christianae, 31(2), pp. 117–25, <doi.org/10.1163/157007277x00284> (accessed 9 November 2022).

12 Brooks, P. (1868), 'O Little Town of Bethlehem' (public domain).

13 Exodus 2.5.

14 Matthew 2.13.

15 Matthew 2.13–23.

16 Exodus 2.15.

17 Exodus 6.28—7.7.

18 Matthew 2.13–21.

19 See Deuteronomy 32.48–52 and Deuteronomy 34 for the last occurrence of mountains in the earthly life of Moses as he approaches his death. Also note that he appears on the Mount of Transfiguration with Jesus in Matthew 17.

20 Matthew 4.8.

21 Matthew 14.23.

22 Matthew 15.29–38.

23 Matthew 24.3.

24 Exodus 12 and 24.1–8.

25 Exodus 34.28.

26 For more on this theme, see Allison, D. C. (1993), *The New Moses: A Matthean Typology* (Minneapolis: Fortress Press), p. 266.

27 Deuteronomy 31.14–29.

28 Deuteronomy 24 and Joshua 1.

29 Deuteronomy 31.23 and Joshua 1.1–9, particularly vv. 5, 7–9.

30 Matthew 28.16–20.

31 Allison, *The New Moses,* p. 261.

32 Deuteronomy 34.6.

33 Matthew 27.45.

34 Matthew 27.51.

35 Matthew 27.51.

36 Matthew 27.52–53.

37 Matthew 5—7.

38 Matthew 10.

39 Matthew 13.

40 Matthew 18.

41 Matthew 22—25.

42 Matthew 5.1-2.

43 Nolland, J. (2005), *The New International Greek Testament Commentary, Volume.1: Matthew* (Grand Rapids: Bletchley: Eerdmans), p. 218.

44 Gaston, L. (2006) *Paul and the Torah* (Eugene: Wipf & Stock), p. 17.

45 For a breathtaking summary of the centrality of Torah in the understanding of Judaism, see Collins, J. J. (2017), *The Invention of Judaism: Torah and Jewish Identity from Deuteronomy to Paul* (Berkeley: University of California Press).

46 Nolland, *The New International Greek Testament Commentary,* p. 218.

47 Matthew 5.18.

48 Matthew 5.19.

49 Matthew 5.17.

50 Nolland, *The New International Greek Testament Commentary,* pp. 218-19.

51 Matthew 5.21-48.

52 Luke 1.33; see also Isaiah 9.7.

53 Matthew 11.3.

54 Not her real name.

55 Hughes, R. K. (2013), *The Sermon on the Mount: The Message of the Kingdom* (Wheaton: Crossway), p. 15. The story is also told, more fully, in Colson, C. W. (1985), *Who Speaks for God? Confronting the World with Real Christianity* (Wheaton: Crossway), p. 153.

56 Harvey, A. E. (1990), *Strenuous Commands: The Ethic of Jesus* (London/Philadelphia: SCM Press), p. 7ff.

57 Yoder, J. H. (2002), *The Politics of Jesus* (Grand Rapids: Eerdmans), pp. 5-7. The inclusion of this reference in no way endorses or supports the wider activity and work of its author. I am aware of the allegations against Yoder, and want to make clear that inclusion of a work by him is not an endorsement of his conduct in any way.

58 I love the full title of Brian McLaren's book, *A Generous Orthodoxy*, which captures for me something of the pervasive nature of Jesus' rule and reign. McLaren, B. D. (2006), *A Generous Orthodoxy: Why*

I Am a Missional, Evangelical, Post/Protestant, Liberal/Conservative, Mystical/Poetic, Biblical, Charismatic/Contemplative, Fundamentalist/ Calvinist, Anabaptist/Anglican, Methodist, Catholic, Green, Incarnational, Depressed-yet-hopeful, Emergent, Unfinished Christian (Grand Rapids: Zondervan).

2 People of the kingdom

1 Day, D. (1952), The *Long Loneliness: The Autobiography of the Legendary Catholic Social Activist* (New York: Curtis Books), p. 44.

2 Not his real name.

3 Pedroza, J. (2022), 'Sparrows Gate | So poor kids can know, love and serve Jesus!', Sparrows Gate Mission, <sparrowsgate.org> (accessed 8 November 2022).

4 Zwick, M. and Zwick, L., 'Dorothy Day and the Catholic Worker Movement', p. 4, in Day, D. (1999), *On Pilgrimage* (Edinburgh/ Grand Rapids: T&T Clark/Eerdmans). The essay provides a wonderful insight into the journey of Day into faith and how she found her place in the Catholic Worker Movement.

5 Day, D. (1938), *From Union Square to Rome* (Silver Spring: Preservation of the Faith Press), p. 6.

6 Day, *The Long Loneliness*, pp. 78–9, 83.

7 Zwick and Zwick, 'Dorothy Day and the Catholic Worker Movement', p. 11.

8 As a reminder, they are in Matthew 5–7; 10; 13; 18; 22—25.

9 I am currently working on a new book exploring the Sermon on the Mount entitled *Higher Call: Life Radically Reimagined through the Sermon on the Mount*. It will be published by SPCK in 2023 and my hope is that it will be the first of a series of five books that explore each of the Matthean discourses in greater detail and depth than can be achieved in *Flipped*.

10 Carson, D. A. (1999), *Jesus' Sermon on the Mount* (Grand Rapids: Baker Books), p. 11.

11 McKnight, S. and Longman III, T. (2013), *Sermon on the Mount: The Story of God Bible Commentary* (Grand Rapids: Zondervan), p. 1.

12 Matthew 5.6.

13 Lloyd-Jones, D. M. (1976), *Studies in the Sermon on the Mount, Volume 1.* 2nd edn (Leicester: Inter-Varsity Press), p. 74.

14 Lapide, P., translated by Swidler, A. (1986), *The Sermon on the Mount: Utopia or Program for Action* (Maryknoll, New York: Orbis Books), p. 4.

15 Bonhoeffer, D. (2004), *The Cost of Discipleship* (London: SCM Press), p. viii.

16 Stott, J. R. W. (1985), *The Message of the Sermon on the Mount* (Leicester: Inter-Varsity Press), p. 15.

17 Willard, D. (1998), *The Divine Conspiracy: Rediscovering Our Hidden Life in God* (New York: HarperCollins).

18 Muggeridge, M. (1975), *Jesus, the Man Who Lives* (London: Collins), p. 61.

19 Carson's two appendices in his work on the Sermon on the Mount are helpful to this end. See Carson, *Jesus' Sermon on the Mount*, pp. 280–99. Greenman, Larson and Spencer's historical overview of how the Sermon on the Mount has been approached is superb. See Greenman, J. P., Larsen, T. and Spencer, S. R. (2007), *The Sermon on the Mount through the Centuries: From the Early Church to John Paul II* (Grand Rapids: Brazos Press). See also Kissinger, W. (1998), *The Sermon on the Mount: A History of Interpretation and Bibliography* (London: Scarecrow), which outlines a history of interpretation of the Sermon and offers an extensive bibliography, which was up to date at the time. Also see Bauman, C. (1990), *The Sermon on the Mount: The Modern Quest for Its Meaning* (Macon: Mercer University Press). Written in 1985, this book explores some of the myriad ways in which the Sermon has been understood. Dale Allison explores the structure of the Sermon and offers interesting insights – see Allison, D. C. (1999), *The Sermon on the Mount: Inspiring the Moral Imagination* (New York: Crossroad). See also Betz, H. D. (2009), *Essays on the Sermon on the Mount* (Minneapolis: Fortress Press); Talbert, C. H. (2004), *Reading the Sermon on the Mount: Character Formation and Decision Making in Matthew 5—7* (Grand Rapids: Baker Academic); Guelich, R. A. (1982), *The Sermon on the Mount: A Foundation for Understanding* (Waco: Word).

For other works that might help in determining your approach to the Sermon, see McKnight and Longman, *Sermon on the Mount*, pp. 1–5, notes 3–11.

20 Much deeper consideration of all of these issues will be included in my forthcoming book, *Higher Call*, mentioned above.

21 Matthew 8.1–4.

22 Matthew 8.5–13.

23 Matthew 8.14–17.

24 Matthew 8.18–22.

25 Matthew 8.23–27.

26 Matthew 8.28–33.

27 Matthew 8.34—9.1.

28 Matthew 9.1–8.

29 Matthew 9.9–13.

30 Matthew 9.14–17.

31 Matthew 9.18–26.

32 Matthew 9.27–31.

33 Matthew 9.32–34.

34 Matthew 9.35–38.

35 Matthew often has miracles witnessed by two people. This is at least in part because he is writing for a Jewish audience and he is proving the legitimacy of Jesus' ministry. In Judaism, two witnesses were required for any claim of the miraculous to be verifiable.

36 Matthew 9.34.

37 Schweller, R. L. (2014), *Maxwell's Demon and the Golden Apple: Global Discord in the New Millennium* (Baltimore: Johns Hopkins University Press), p. 1.

38 Micklethwait, J. and Wooldridge, A. (2020), *The Wake-up Call: Why the Pandemic Has Exposed the Weakness of the West – and How to Fix it* (London: Short Books), p. 19.

39 Sayers, M. (2022), *A Non-anxious Presence: How a Changing and Complex World Will Create a Remnant of Renewed Christian Leaders* (Chicago: Moody Publishers), p. 22.

40 Matthew 4.23–25; 9.35.

41 Kyria Network, <kyrianetwork.com> (accessed 8 November 2022).

42 Matthew 26.7; Mark 14.3; Luke 7.37.

43 Not her real name.

44 Diocese of London, 'New-Monastic Living on an Ancient Pathway' (2022), <www.london.anglican.org/articles/new-monastic-living-on-an-ancient-pathway> (accessed 9 November 2022).

45 Vanessa Elston, cited in Diocese of London, 'New-Monastic Living on an Ancient Pathway'.

46 Vanessa Elston, cited in Diocese of London, 'New-Monastic Living on an Ancient Pathway'.

3 The purpose of the kingdom

1 Jordan, J. B. (1988), *Through New Eyes: Developing a Biblical View of the World* (Brentwood: Wolgemuth Hyatt), pp. 42, 47.

2 For more information about Jackie's ministry, see 'About Us', St Stephen's Society, <www.ststephenssociety.com/en/aboutus.php> (accessed 8 November 2022).

3 Pan was the Greek God of the wild, of the impromptu and of shepherds, among other things. The city was variously named Panion or Paneas in his honour. For a fascinating overview of the city, see Wilson, J. F. (2004), *Caesarea Philippi: Banias, the Lost City of Pan* (London: I. B. Tauris).

4 Josephus, F. (2010), *The Works of Flavius Josephus Containing Twenty Books of the Jewish Antiquities, Seven Books of the Jewish War and the Life of Josephus* (Memphis: General Books). Volume 15, pp. 363–4.

5 Burgess, J. A. (1976), *A History of the Exegesis of Matthew 16:17–19 from 1781 to 1965* (Ann Arbor: Edwards Brothers). Nickelsburg, G. W. E. (1981), 'Enoch, Levi, and Peter: Recipients of Revelation in Upper Galilee', *Journal of Biblical Literature*, 100(4), pp. 575–600, <doi.org/10.2307/3266120> (accessed 8 November 2022).

6 See Davies, W. D. and Allison, D. C. (1991), *A Critical and Exegetical Commentary on the Gospel According to Saint Matthew: In 3 Volumes* (Edinburgh: T&T Clark), Volume 2, p. 602.

7 Riggle, H. M. (1917), *Roman Catholicism in the Light of Their Own Scriptures and Authorities* (Anderson: Gospel Trumpet Company), pp. 51–2.

8 Gibbons, J. (1907), *The Faith of Our Fathers: Being a Plain Exposition and Vindication of the Church Founded by Our Lord Jesus Christ* (Baltimore: J. Murphy), p. 95.

9 For a summary of some of this discussion, see Hendriksen, W. (1989), *The Gospel of Matthew* (Edinburgh: Banner of Truth Trust), pp. 644–51.

10 Acts 3.12–13; 4.12; 1 Corinthians 3.1, for example.

11 1 Corinthians 15.6.

12 Matthew 28.19.

13 Philippians 2.5.

14 Ephesians 2.1–10.

15 2 Corinthians 5.17.

16 Galatians 2.20.

17 Philippians 1.21.

18 Matthew 10.7.

19 It appears around 61 times in the New Testament, including nine times in Matthew. For a full list of usage in the New Testament, see <www.stepbible.org/?q=version=ESV|strong=G2784&options=NVHUG&qFilter=G2784> (accessed 8 November 2022).

20 Matthew 3.1.

21 Matthew 4.17, 23; 9.35; 11.1.

22 Matthew 10.7, 27; 24.14; 26.13.

23 The word is used eight times in Acts – see 8.5; 9.20; 10.37, 42; 15.21; 19.13; 20.25; 28.31.

24 For example, see Romans 2.21; 10.8, 14, 15; 1 Corinthians 1.23; 9.27; 15.11, 12; 2 Corinthians 1.19; 4.5; 11.4; Galatians 2.2; Philippians 1.15; Colossians 1.23; 1 Thessalonians 2.9; 1 Timothy 3.16 and 2 Timothy 4.2.

25 1 Peter 3.19.

26 Revelation 5.2.

27 For example, see Pilavachi, M. and Hoeksma, L. (2006), *When Necessary, Use Words: Changing Lives through Worship, Justice and Evangelism* (Ventura: Regal Books). In fact, St Francis never suggested that words were unimportant; rather, he argued that they must be accompanied by evidence of a life committed to the message being spoken.

28 2 Corinthians 5.19; Colossians 1.15–23.

29 See Matthew 4.23; 9.35, for example.

30 Isaiah 61.1–3; Luke 4.16–21.

31 For example, John 2.11; 20.30.

32 Matthew 25.31–46.

33 Matthew 11.28–30.

34 For example, see Matthew 13, where seven such parables can be found.

4 The perspective of the kingdom

1 For more information, contact Manna 4 Many, 140 North Queen Street, Belfast, BT15 1HQ. Tel 07747 683360. See also its Facebook page: <www.facebook.com/Manna-4-Many-Street-Aid-364756340574813> (accessed 9 November 2022).

2 Matthew 5.3–12.

3 Matthew 5.13–16.

4 Matthew 5.17–21.

5 Matthew 5.21–47.

6 Matthew 5.48.

7 Matthew 5.3–12.

8 As well as using it in Matthew 5.3, 4, 5, 6, 7, 8, 9, 10, 11 the gospel writer uses it in 11.6; 13.16; 16.17 and 24.46. Each one is significant in helping us understand the message of Jesus in Matthew. Matthew 11.6 links to not taking offence at the teaching and message of Jesus. Matthew 13.16 is connected with those who truly see and understand the message of Christ. Matthew 16.17 is the blessing associated with Simon Peter in his confession of Christ as the Messiah, and Matthew 24.46 is connected with faithfulness to God and God's purposes for our lives.

9 Matthew 5.3.

10 Matthew 5.4.

11 Matthew 5.5.

12 Matthew 5.6.

13 Matthew 5.7.

14 Matthew 5.8.

15 Matthew 5.9.

16 Matthew 5.10.

17 Matthew 4.23–35; 9.35.

18 See Luke 6.20–26.

19 Warner, R. (1998), *Sermon on the Mount* (Eastbourne: Kingsway Publications), p. 41.

20 Matthew 5.1.

21 Isaiah 42.3, Matthew 12.20. See also Psalm 34.18 and the invitation of Jesus in Matthew 11.28–30.

22 Psalm 107.9.

23 Psalm 34.8.

24 Matthew 11.28.

25 John 6.37.

26 Luke 7.47.

27 Stott, J. R. W. (1985), *The Message of the Sermon on the Mount* (Leicester: Inter-Varsity Press), pp. 69–81; Lloyd-Jones, D. M. (1976), *Studies in the Sermon on the Mount, Volume 1* (Leicester: Inter-Varsity Press), pp. 149–79.

28 See 'King Jesus, Moses and Torah' in chapter 1, 'King of the kingdom'.

29 See 'King Jesus, Moses and Torah' in chapter 1, 'King of the kingdom'.

30 Matthew 5.21–26.

31 Matthew 5.27–30.

32 Matthew 5.31–32.

33 Matthew 5.33–37.

34 Matthew 5.38–42.

35 Matthew 5.43–47.

36 Matthew 5.21–22, 27–28, 31–32, 33–34, 38–39, 43–44.

37 See Proverbs 23.7, for example, which states, 'For as he thinks in his heart, so *is* he' (NKJV). For a fascinating article exploring the different ways in which this verse could have been understood, see Baker, K. L. (1989), 'Proverbs 23: "To Think" or "To Serve Food?"', *Journal of Ancient Near Eastern Society*, 19(1), p. 2345.

38 He returns to this very issue in Matthew 23, when he publicly

challenges the mindset, legalism and double standards of the Pharisees.

39 See also Exodus 21.23–25; Leviticus 24.19–20; Deuteronomy 19.21 and Obadiah 15 for some of the scriptural context of these words.

40 For an exploration of the whole issue of *lex talionis* and the way Jesus redefines it here, see McKnight, S. and Longman III, T. (2013), *Sermon on the Mount: The Story of God Bible Commentary* (Grand Rapids: Zondervan), pp. 138–54.

41 Matthew 6.1–4.

42 Matthew 6.5–15.

43 Matthew 6.16–18.

44 Matthew 6.19–21, 24.

45 Matthew 6.25–34.

46 Matthew 6.22–23.

47 Matthew 7.1–5.

48 Matthew 7.6.

49 Matthew 7.7–11.

50 Luke 11.13.

51 Matthew 7.1-14.

52 Matthew 7.15–20.

53 Matthew 7.21–23.

54 Matthew 7.24–27.

5 The promise of the kingdom

1 'What We Do', Cornerstone Baptist Church, <www. cornerstonedallas.org/what-we-do> (accessed 9 November 2022).

2 Matthew 20.16.

3 For example, Dand, S. (2021), 'New grocery store reflects Cornerstone church's belief that "South Dallas deserves beautiful things"', <dallasfreepress.com/south-dallas/new-grocery-store -reflects-cornerstone-churchs-belief-that-south-dallas-deserves -beautiful-things> (accessed 9 November 2022).

4 2 Corinthians 12.9.

5 Green, M. (2000), *The Message of Matthew* (Nottingham: Inter-Varsity Press), p. 43.

6 For example, Matthew 23—24.

7 Willard, D. and Black, G. (2014) *The Divine Conspiracy Continued: Fulfilling God's Kingdom on Earth* (London: HarperCollins), p. 5.

8 Hill, C. (1991), *The World Turned Upside Down: Radical Ideas During the English Revolution* (Harmondsworth: Penguin Books).

9 Hill, *The World Turned Upside Down*, p. 97.

10 Sayers, M. (2014), *Facing Leviathan: Leadership, Influence, and Creating in a Cultural Storm* (Chicago: Moody Publishers), p. 217.

11 Duncan, M. (2013), *Risk Takers: The Life God Intends for You* (Oxford: Monarch Books).

12 Matthew 4.1–11.

13 Genesis 25.29–32.

14 Matthew 5.14 (THE MESSAGE).

15 Schaeffer, F. A. (1986), *The Great Evangelical Disaster* (Westchester: Crossway), pp. 37–8.

16 Blackaby, H. T. and Blackaby, R. (2011), *Spiritual Leadership: Moving People on to God's Agenda* (Nashville: B&H Publishing Group), p. 40.

17 Wright, T. (2012), *How God Became King: Getting to the Heart of the Gospels* (London: SPCK), p. 276.

Bibliography

1 The inclusion of this source in no way endorses or supports the wider activity and work of its author. I am aware of the allegations against Yoder, and want to make clear that inclusion of a work by him is not an endorsement of his conduct in any way.

Bibliography

Allison, D. C. (1993) *The New Moses: A Matthean Typology*. Minneapolis: Fortress Press.

Allison, D. C. (1999) *The Sermon on the Mount: Inspiring the Moral Imagination*. New York: Crossroad.

Baker, K. L. (1989) 'Proverbs 23: "To Think" or "To Serve Food?"', *Journal of Ancient Near Eastern Society*, 19(1).

Bauman, C. (1990) *The Sermon on the Mount: The Modern Quest for Its Meaning*. Macon: Mercer University Press.

Betz, H. D. (2009) *Essays on the Sermon on the Mount*. Minneapolis: Fortress Press.

Blackaby, H. T. and Blackaby, R. (2011) *Spiritual Leadership: Moving People on to God's Agenda*. Nashville: B&H Publishing Group.

Bonhoeffer, D. (2004) *The Cost of Discipleship*. London: SCM Press.

Bown, D. (2019) *Kingdom People: How We Created Spiritual and Social Renewal in a Marginalised Society*. Darlington: McKnight & Bishop Inspire.

Brooks, P. (2010) 'O Little Town of Bethlehem' (public domain).

Bruns, J. E. (1977) 'The "Agreement of Moses and Jesus" in the "Demonstratio Evangelica" of Eusebius', *Vigiliae Christianae*, 31(2). <doi.org/10.1163/157007277x00284>.

Burgess, J. A. (1976) *A History of the Exegesis of Matthew 16:17–19 from 1781 to 1965*. Ann Arbor: Edwards Brothers.

Carson, D. A. (1999) *Jesus' Sermon on the Mount*. Grand Rapids: Baker Books.

Chrupcała, L. (2022) 'The Kingdom of God: A Bibliography of 20th Century Research. Update', *Academia.edu*. <www.academia.edu /41346521/The_Kingdom_of_God_A_Bibliography_of_20th _Century_Research._Update>.

Collins, J. J. (2017) *The Invention of Judaism: Torah and Jewish Identity from Deuteronomy to Paul*. Berkeley: University of California Press.

Colson, C. W. (1985) *Who Speaks for God? Confronting the World with Real Christianity.* Wheaton: Crossway.

Cornerstone Baptist Church (2022), 'What We Do'. <www.cornerstonedallas.org/what-we-do>.

Dand, S. (2021) 'New grocery store reflects Cornerstone church's belief that "South Dallas deserves beautiful things"', *Dallas Free Press.* <dallasfreepress.com/south-dallas/new-grocery-store-reflects -cornerstone-churchs-belief-that-south-dallas-deserves-beautiful-things>.

Davies, W. D. and Allison, D. C. (1991) *A Critical and Exegetical Commentary on the Gospel According to Saint Matthew: In 3 Volumes.* Edinburgh: T&T Clark.

Day, D. (1938) *From Union Square to Rome.* Silver Spring: Preservation of the Faith Press.

Day, D. (1952) *The Long Loneliness: The Autobiography of the Legendary Catholic Social Activist.* New York: Curtis Books.

Day, D. (1999) *On Pilgrimage.* Edinburgh/Grand Rapids: T&T Clark/ Eerdmans.

Diocese of London. 'New-Monastic Living on an Ancient Pathway' (2022). <www.london.anglican.org/articles/new-monastic-living -on-an-ancient-pathway>.

Diocese of Worcester (2022) 'Kingdom People'. <www.cofe-worcester .org.uk/kingdom-people>.

Duncan, M. (2013) *Risk Takers: The Life God Intends for You.* Oxford: Monarch Books.

Fairbairn, A. M. (1893) *The Place of Christ in Modern Theology.* 2nd edn. London: Hodder & Stoughton.

Faith and Order Commission, The (2020) *Kingdom Calling: The Vocation, Ministry and Discipleship of the Whole People of God.* London: Church House Publishing.

Gaston, L. (2006) *Paul and the Torah.* Eugene: Wipf & Stock.

Gibbons, J. (1907) *The Faith of Our Fathers: Being a Plain Exposition and Vindication of the Church Founded by Our Lord Jesus Christ.* Baltimore: J. Murphy.

Gladden, W. (1894) *The Church and the Kingdom.* New York: Fleming H. Revell.

Green, M. (2000) *The Message of Matthew*. Nottingham: Inter-Varsity Press.

Greenman, J. P., Larsen, T. and Spencer, S. R. (2007) *The Sermon on the Mount through the Centuries: From the Early Church to John Paul II*. Grand Rapids: Brazos Press.

Guelich, R. A. (1982) *The Sermon on the Mount: A Foundation for Understanding*. Waco: Word.

Gutiérrez, G., translated by Inda, C. and Eagleson, J. (1973) *A Theology of Liberation: History, Politics, and Salvation*. Maryknoll, New York: Orbis Books.

Gutiérrez G., translated by O'Connell, M. J. (1984) *We Drink from Our Own Wells: The Spiritual Journey of a People*. Maryknoll, New York: Orbis Books.

Gutiérrez G., translated by O'Connell, M. J. (1991) *The God of Life*. Maryknoll, New York: Orbis Books.

Harvey, A. E. (1990) *Strenuous Commands: The Ethic of Jesus*. London/ Philadelphia: SCM Press.

Heli, Tibur (2016) 'Encountering God in the Face of the Poor According to Gustavo Gutierrez," 南山神学, 39, pp. 159–79.

Hendriksen, W. (1989) *The Gospel of Matthew*. Edinburgh: Banner of Truth Trust.

Hill, C. (1991) *The World Turned Upside Down: Radical Ideas During the English Revolution*. Harmondsworth: Penguin Books.

Huddleston, T. (1956) *Naught for Your Comfort*. London: Collins.

Hughes., R. K. (2013) *The Sermon on the Mount: The Message of the Kingdom*. Wheaton: Crossway.

Jenkins, D. (2013) *Kingdom People Living by Kingdom Principles: A Holistic Approach to the Call of Missions*. Bloomington: Westbow Press.

Jordan, J. B. (1988) *Through New Eyes: Developing a Biblical View of the World*. Brentwood: Wolgemuth Hyatt.

Josephus, F. (2010), *The Works of Flavius Josephus Containing Twenty Books of the Jewish Antiquities, Seven Books of the Jewish War and the Life of Josephus*. Memphis: General Books.

Kissinger, W. S. (1998) *The Sermon on the Mount: A History of Interpretation and Bibliography*. London: Scarecrow.

Kyria Network. <kyrianetwork.com>.

Ladd, G. E. (1966) *Jesus and the Kingdom: Scriptural Studies in the Kingdom of God*. London: SPCK.

Lapide, P., translated by A. Swidler (1986) *The Sermon on the Mount: Utopia or Program for Action*. Maryknoll, New York: Orbis Books.

Lewis, C. S. (1982) *The Screwtape Letters*. New York: Bantam Books.

Lewis, C. S. (2009) *The Magician's Nephew (The Chronicles of Narnia, Book 1)*. London: HarperCollins Publishers.

Lewis, C. S. (2012) *That Hideous Strength*. New York: Harper One.

Lierman, J. (2004) *The New Testament Moses: Christian Perceptions of Moses and Israel in the Setting of Jewish Religion*. Tübingen: Mohr Siebeck.

Linney, G. (2022) 'Thinking Anew – Love Is Stronger Than Hate', *Irish Times*. <www.irishtimes.com/news/social-affairs/religion-and -beliefs/thinking-anew-love-is-stronger-than-hate-1.4778712#:~: text=At%20the%20core%20of%20who,through%20Him%20who %20loves%20us>.

Lloyd-Jones, D. M. (1976) *Studies in the Sermon on the Mount, Volume 1*. 2nd edn. Leicester: Inter-Varsity Press.

McKnight, S. and Longman III, T. (2013) *Sermon on the Mount: The Story of God Bible Commentary*. Grand Rapids: Zondervan.

McLaren, B. D. (2006) *A Generous Orthodoxy: Why I Am a Missional, Evangelical, Post/Protestant, Liberal/Conservative, Mystical/Poetic, Biblical, Charismatic/Contemplative, Fundamentalist/Calvinist, Anabaptist/Anglican, Methodist, Catholic, Green, Incarnational, Depressed-yet-hopeful, Emergent, Unfinished Christian*. Grand Rapids: Zondervan.

Meeks, W. A., edited by Van Unnik, W. C. (1967) *The Prophet-King: Moses Traditions and the Johannine Christology*. Supplements to Novum Testamentum. Leiden: E. J. Brill.

Micklethwait, J. and Wooldridge, A. (2020) *The Wake-up Call: Why the Pandemic Has Exposed the Weakness of the West – and How to Fix It*. London: Short Books.

Muggeridge, M. (1975) *Jesus, the Man Who Lives*. London: Collins.

Nickelsburg, G. W. E. (1981) 'Enoch, Levi, and Peter: Recipients of Revelation in Upper Galilee', *Journal of Biblical Literature*, 100(4), pp. 575–600. <doi.org/10.2307/3266120>.

Nolland, J. (2005) *The New International Greek Testament Commentary, Volume 1: Matthew*. Grand Rapids: Bletchley: Eerdmans.

Pedroza, J. (2022) 'Sparrows Gate | So poor kids can know, love and serve Jesus!', Sparrows Gate Mission. <sparrowsgate.org>.

Pilavachi, M. and Hoeksma, L. (2006) *When Necessary, Use Words: Changing Lives through Worship, Justice and Evangelism*. Ventura: Regal Books.

Porter, J. R. (1963) *Moses and Monarchy: A Study in the Biblical Tradition of Moses*. Oxford: Blackwell.

Pullinger, J. (2022) 'About Us', St Stephen's Society. <www.ststephenssociety.com/en/aboutus.php>.

Riggle, H. M. (1917) *Roman Catholicism in the Light of Their Own Scriptures and Authorities*. Anderson: Gospel Trumpet Company.

Sayers, M. (2014) *Facing Leviathan: Leadership, Influence, and Creating in a Cultural Storm*. Chicago: Moody Publishers.

Sayers, M. (2022) *A Non-anxious Presence: How a Changing and Complex World Will Create a Remnant of Renewed Christian Leaders*. Chicago: Moody Publishers.

Schaeffer, F. A. (1986) *The Great Evangelical Disaster*. Westchester: Crossway.

Schweller, R. L. (2014) *Maxwell's Demon and the Golden Apple: Global Discord in the New Millennium*. Baltimore: Johns Hopkins University Press.

Sproul, R. C. (2017) *The R. C. Sproul Collection, Volume 2*. Carol Stream: Tyndale House Publishers, Inc.

Stott, J. R. W. (1985) *The Message of the Sermon on the Mount*. Leicester: Inter-Varsity Press.

Talbert, C. H. (2004) *Reading the Sermon on the Mount: Character Formation and Decision Making in Matthew 5—7.*, Grand Rapids: Baker Academic.

Townend, S., Getty, K. and Getty, K. (2022) 'Hear the Call of the Kingdom'. <www.stuarttownend.co.uk/song/hear-the-call-of-the-kingdom>.

Tutu, D. (1995) *An African Prayer Book*. New York: Doubleday.

Tutu, D., Mutloatse, M. and Webster, J. (1984) *Hope and Suffering*. Glasgow: Collins Fount.

Veith, G. E. (2005) *Soul of the Lion, the Witch, and the Wardrobe.* Colorado Springs: Victor.

Vineyard USA (2022), 'What Is the Kingdom: How Do We Become Kingdom People?' <vineyardusa.org/library/what-is-the-kingdom -how-do-we-become-kingdom-people>.

Warner, R. (1998) *Sermon on the Mount.* Eastbourne: Kingsway Publications.

Willard, D. (1998) *The Divine Conspiracy: Rediscovering Our Hidden Life in God.* New York: HarperCollins.

Willard, D. and Black, G. (2014) *The Divine Conspiracy Continued: Fulfilling God's Kingdom on Earth.* London: HarperCollins.

Wilson, J. F. (2004) *Caesarea Philippi: Banias, the Lost City of Pan.* London: I. B. Tauris.

Wright, D. (2022) 'Christians Are Called to Be a Kingdom People'. Vineyard Churches. >www.vineyardchurches.org.uk/resources /christians-are-called-to-be-a-kingdom-people>.

Wright, T. (2012) *How God Became King: Getting to the Heart of the Gospels.* London: SPCK.

Yoder, J. H. (2002) *The Politics of Jesus.* Grand Rapids: Eerdmans.[1]

Copyright acknowledgements

The publisher and author acknowledge with thanks permission to reproduce extracts from the following:

The Screwtape Letters by C. S. Lewis copyright © C. S. Lewis Pte Ltd 1942. Extract reprinted by permission.

Every effort has been made to seek permission to use copyright material reproduced in this book. The publisher apologizes for those cases where permission might not have been sought and, if notified, will formally seek permission at the earliest opportunity.

Unless otherwise noted, Scripture quotations are taken from the New Revised Standard Version of the Bible, Anglicized Edition, copyright © 1989, 1995 by the Division of Christian Education of the National Council of the Churches of Christ in the USA. Used by permission. All rights reserved.

Quotations marked KJV are taken from the Authorized Version of the Bible (The King James Bible), the rights in which are vested in the Crown, and are reproduced by permission of the Crown's Patentee, Cambridge University Press.

Quotations marked THE MESSAGE are from *THE MESSAGE*. Copyright © by Eugene H. Peterson 1993, 1994, 1995, 1996, 2000, 2001, 2002. Used by permission of NavPress Publishing Group.

Quotations marked NIV are taken from The Holy Bible, New International Version (Anglicized edition). Copyright © 1979, 1984, 2011 by Biblica. Used by permission of Hodder & Stoughton Ltd, an Hachette UK company. All rights reserved. 'NIV' is a registered trademark of Biblica. UK trademark number 1448790.

Quotations marked NKJV are taken from the New King James Version. Copyright © 1982 by Thomas Nelson, Inc. Used by permission. All rights reserved.

Quotations marked NLT are taken from the *Holy Bible*, New Living Translation, copyright © 1996. Used by permission of Tyndale House Publishers, Inc., Carol Stream, Illinois 60189, USA. All rights reserved.

OTHER BOOKS
BY MALCOLM DUNCAN

MALCOLM DUNCAN

GOOD
GRIEF

LIVING WIT...
SORROW AND...

COMING
SOON

MALCOLM DUNCAN

Niteblessings

Meditations to close the day

...LM DUNCAN

TO FIND OUT MORE ABOUT THE NEXT
BOOK FROM MALCOLM DUNCAN,
FOLLOW HIM ON

  @MALCOLMJDUNCAN

 spck publishing

INTERACTIVE BIBLE STUDIES FOR GROUP AND INDIVIDUAL USE THAT HELP YOU DISCOVER THE BEAUTY OF LIVING OUT JESUS' BEATITUDES

THE OFFICIAL WORKBOOK FOR
SPRING HARVEST 2023

9780281088140 | PAPERBACK & EBOOK | 80 PAGES

spck publishing